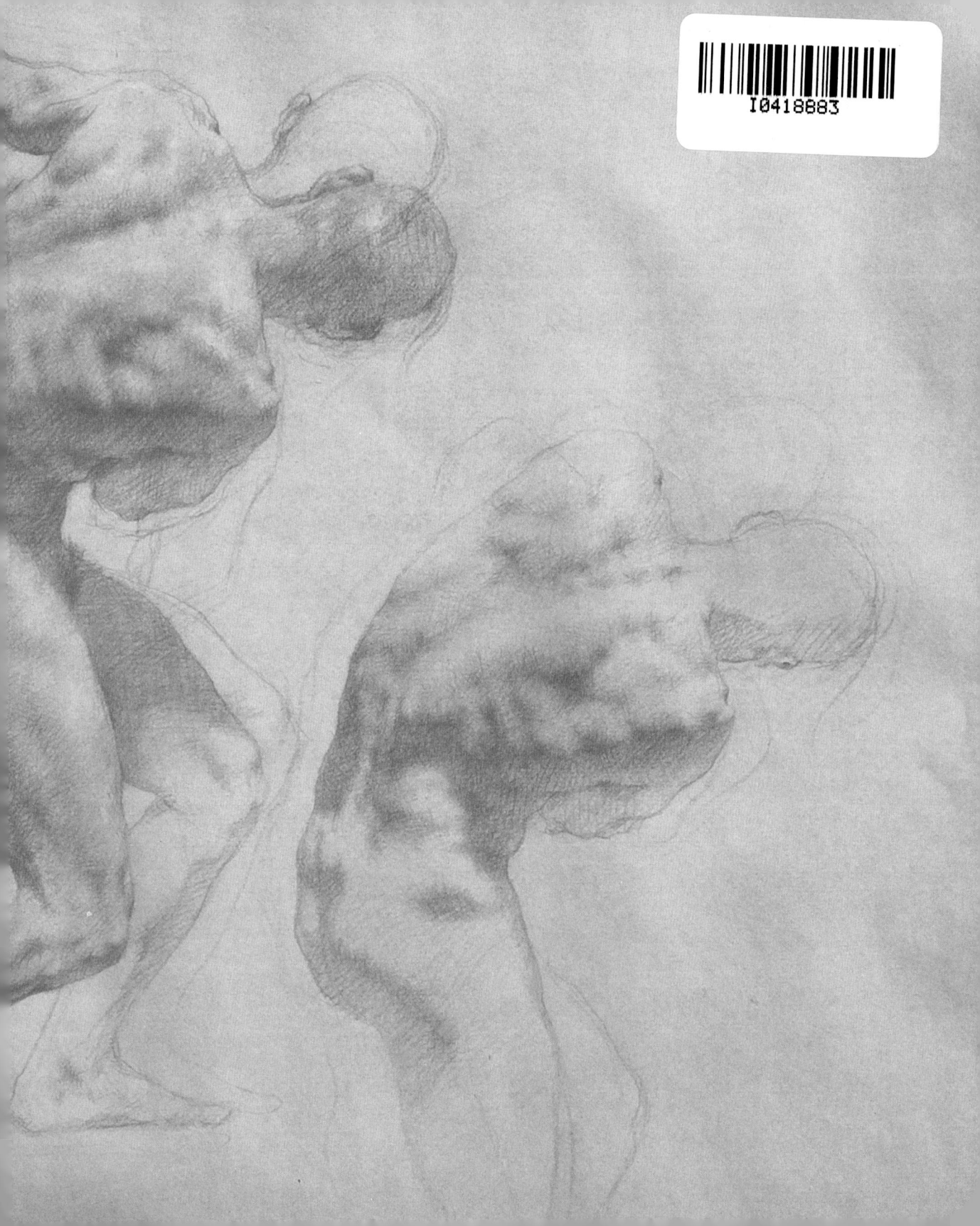

FIGURE
DRAWING
ATELIER

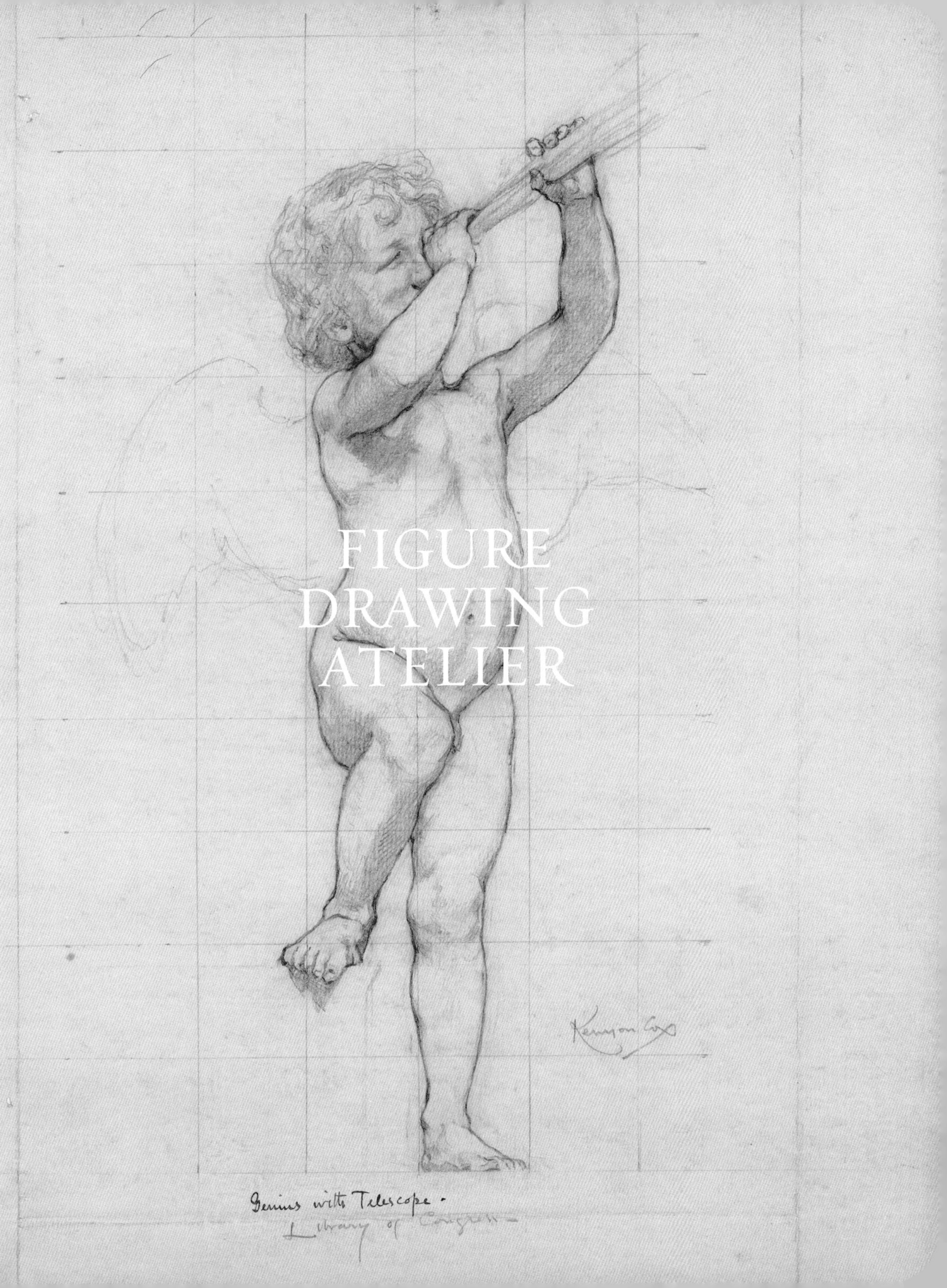

Genius with Telescope -
Library of Congress

Kenyon Cox

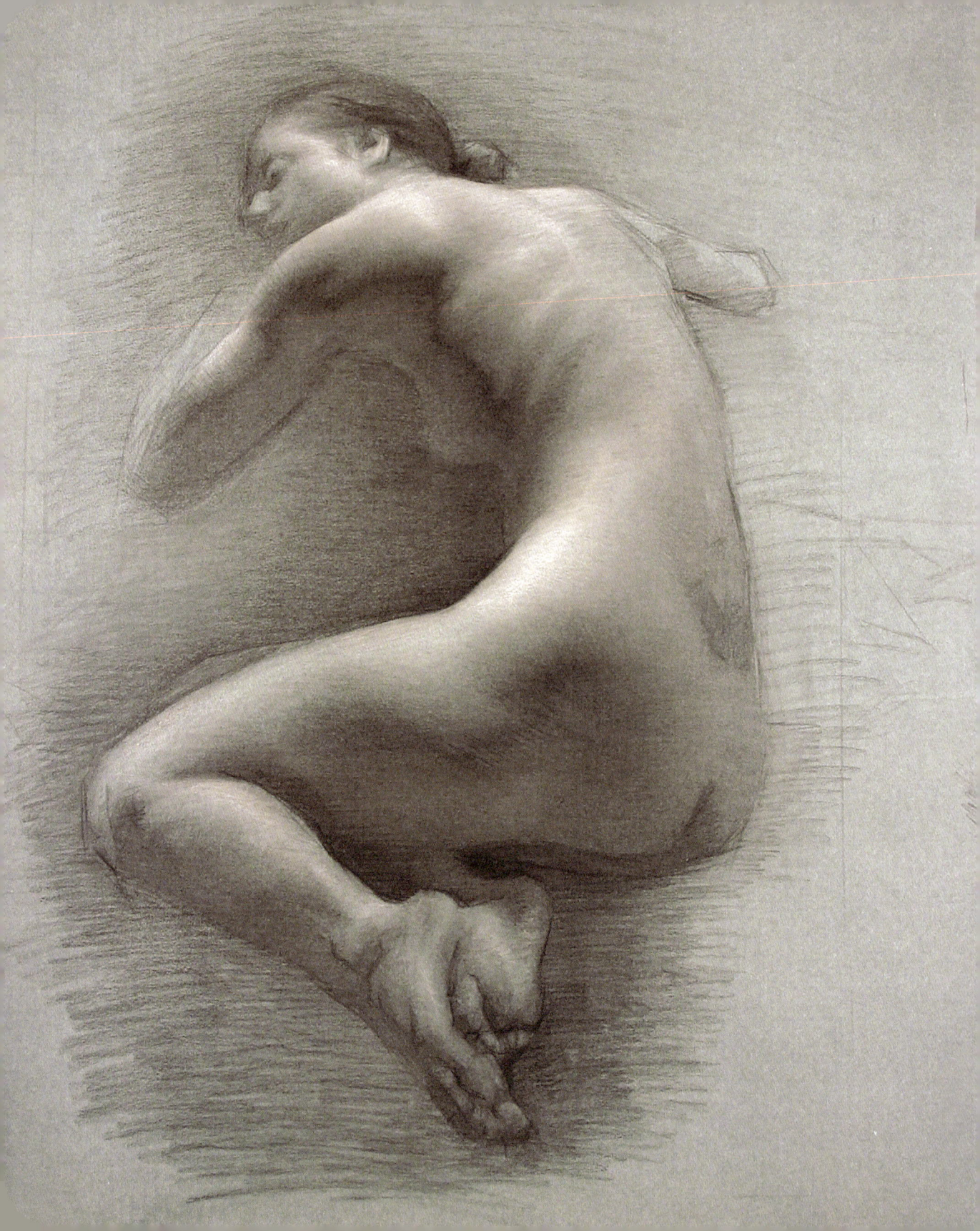

FIGURE DRAWING ATELIER

An Instructional Sketchbook

Juliette Aristides

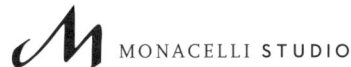
MONACELLI STUDIO

Copyright © 2019 Juliette Aristides and The Monacelli Press
Illustrations copyright © 2019 Juliette Aristides unless otherwise noted
Text copyright © 2019 Juliette Aristides

Published in the United States by Monacelli Studio, an imprint of The Monacelli Press

All rights reserved.

Library of Congress Cataloging-in-Publication Data

Names: Aristides, Juliette, author.
Title: Figure drawing atelier : an instructional sketchbook / by Juliette Aristides.
Description: First edition. | New York : Monacelli Studio, 2019
Identifiers: LCCN 2018026414 | ISBN 9781580935135 (hardback)
Subjects: LCSH: Figure drawing--Technique. | Human figure in art. | BISAC:
ART / Techniques / Life Drawing. | ART / Subjects & Themes / Human Figure.
| ART / Techniques / Drawing.
Classification: LCC NC765 .A75 2018 | DDC 741.09/04--dc23
LC record available at https://lccn.loc.gov/2018026414

ISBN 978-1-58093-513-5

Printed in China

Design by Jennifer K. Beal Davis
Cover design by Jennifer K. Beal Davis
Cover illustrations by Candice Bohannon (front) and Edgar Degas (back)
Endpapers by Robert Liberace

10 9 8 7 6 5

Monacelli Studio
The Monacelli Press
111 Broadway
New York, New York 10006
www.monacellipress.com

CREDITS

Endpapers: Michael Mentler, *From the Sketchbook*, 2007, ink wash, pen, and gouache heightened with white, 12 x 9 inches (30.5 x 22.9 cm)

Page 1: Kenyon Cox, *Genius with Telescope*, ca. 1896, graphite on paper, size unknown, Library of Congress

Page 2: Juliette Aristides, *Rest*, 2014, charcoal on blue-toned paper heightened with white, 24 x 18 inches (61x 45.7 cm)

Page 5: Candice Bohannon, *Pleading Heart*, 2015, mixed media on Mylar, 15 x 17 ½ inches (38.1 x 44.4 cm)

Page 6: Alexey Steele, *The Distant Fire on a Full Moon*, 2013, charcoal on toned paper heightened with white, 19 x 15 inches (48.3 x 38 cm)

To you, the artist

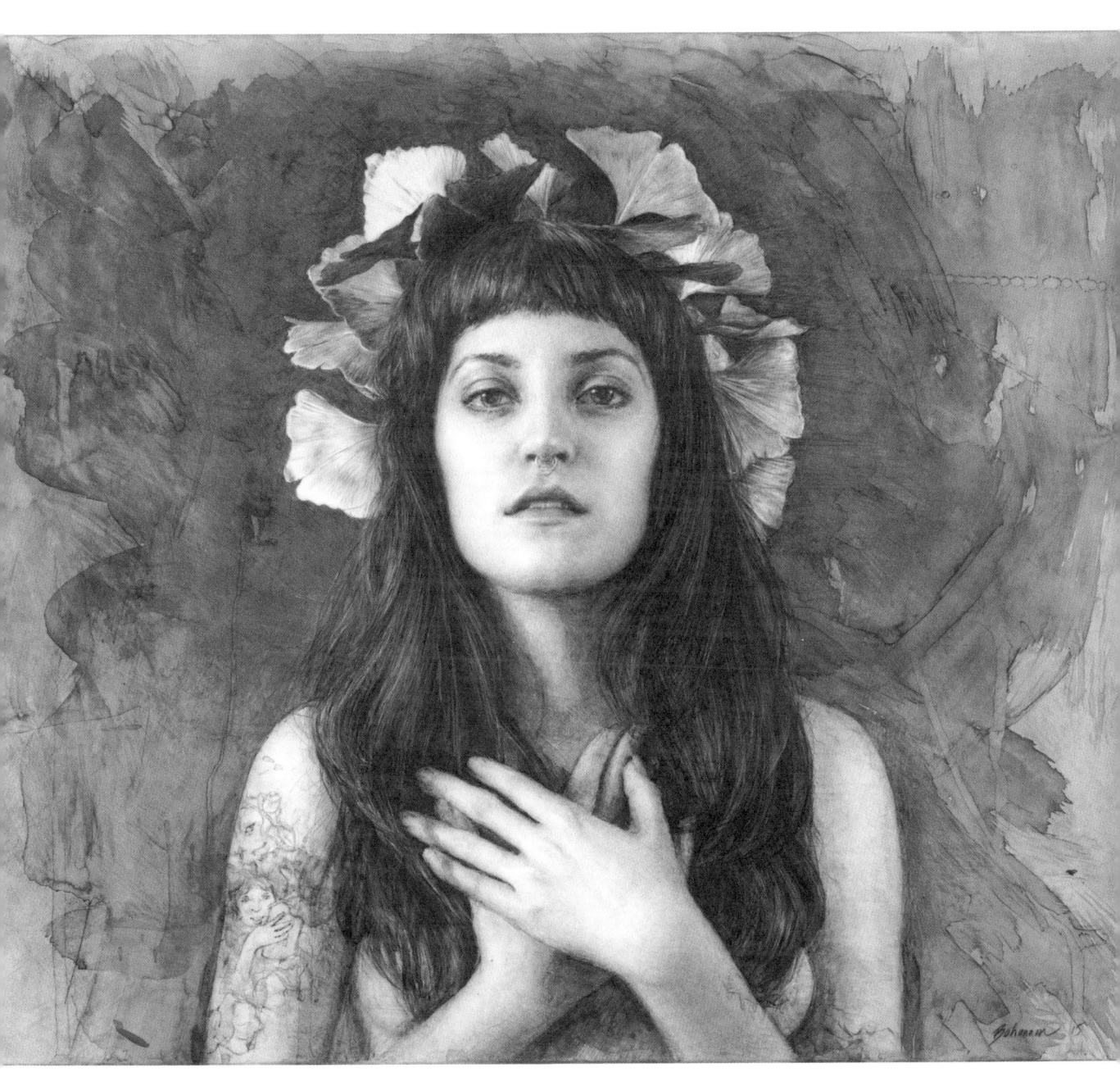

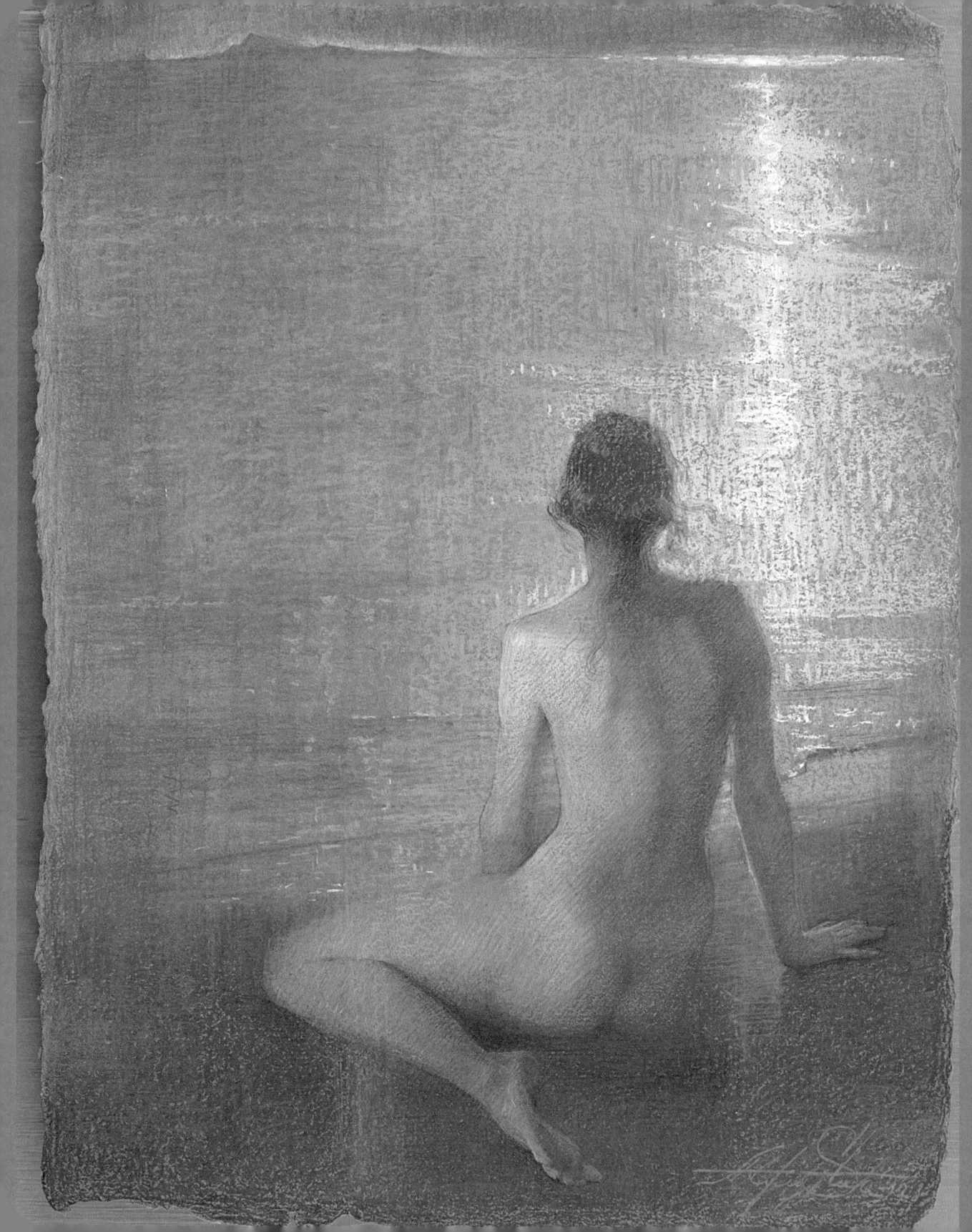

CONTENTS

Opening 8

1 THE LINE OF ACTION 16

2 THE BLOCK-IN 34

3 VOLUME 52

4 HEADS, HANDS, AND FEET 68

5 VALUE AND FORM 90

6 MASTER STUDIO 116

Closing 122

Acknowledgments 126

Index 127

About the Author 128

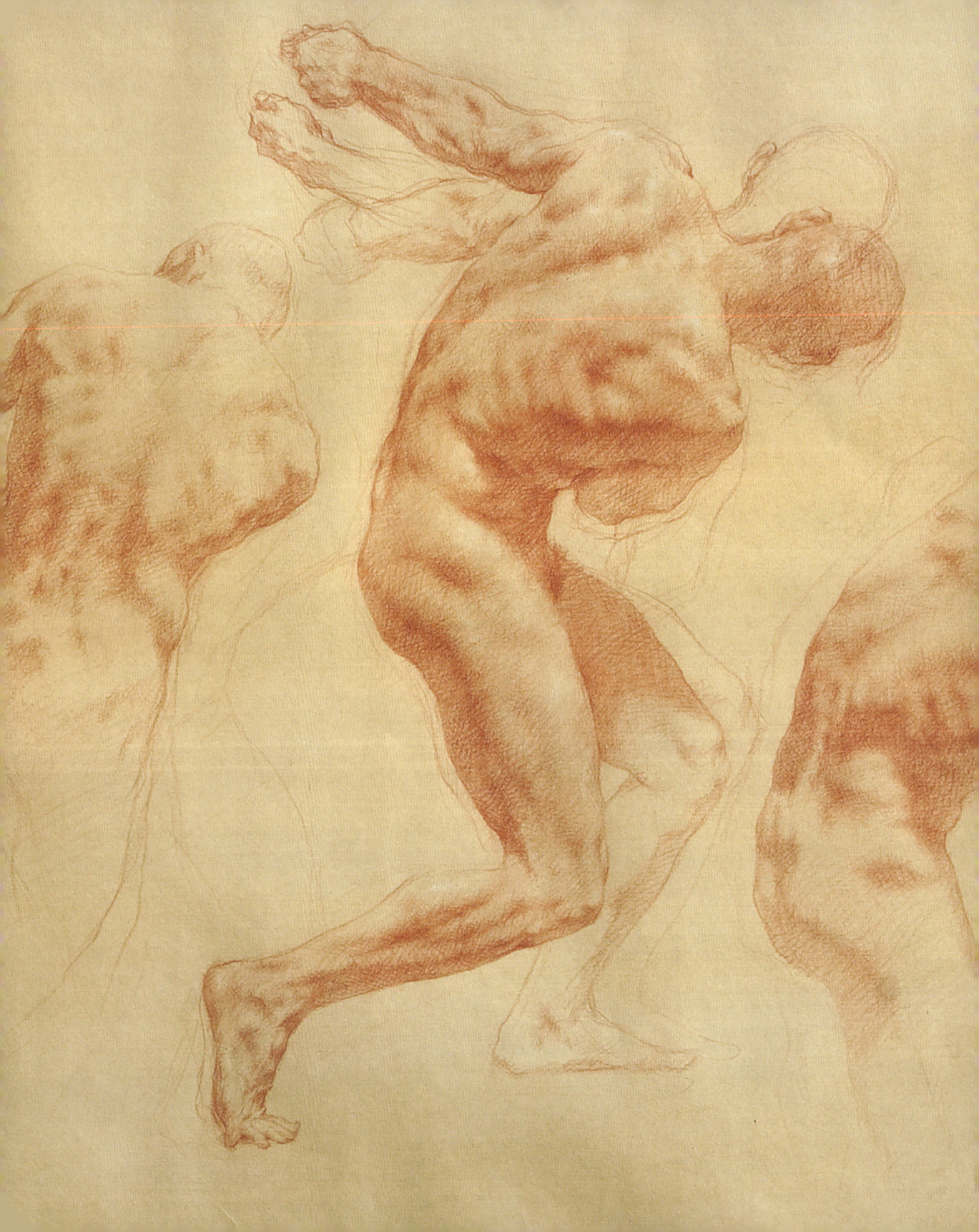

OPENING

All the past up to a moment ago is your legacy. You have a right to it.
The works of ancient masters, those of the student next to you, the remark
let drop a moment ago; all is experience.

—ROBERT HENRI, *THE ART SPIRIT*

The history of art in the Western world is inseparable from its principal subject: the human figure. Over the centuries, women and men have modeled in an endless parade of mythological, historical, religious, and portrait paintings. Supporting this stream of production were the studios, guilds, and academies that trained artists to master the human form. Much has changed in the world, yet the figure remains central to artistic expression—probably because, as artist Gary Faigin observed, a face is the most important thing in the world to a human being. Our shared identity as human beings forms the most basic link between artist and viewer.

When we pursue skills in figure drawing, we don't journey alone; we join the ranks of past artists and are aided by a storehouse of knowledge many simply call "the tradition." This body of information accumulated slowly through the combined efforts of centuries of practitioners. The tradition gives us a common language with which to understand art of the past and, as we add our voices, create new art for our own times.

In this book, you will study the same proven methods that helped train artists of the past. Most artists began their studies by copying the work of master draftsmen to learn the secrets of their success. The most important part of your art education is the basic skills learned in the beginning. During my student years, I took the same foundation drawing classes multiple times to gain the strongest possible understanding.

OPPOSITE: Robert Liberace, *Figure Pulling* (detail), 2010, red chalk on paper, 18 x 30 inches (45.7 x 76.2 cm)

When learning to draw the nude, many people are unsure how to start. In real life, naked people are usually nothing like what we see in films, fashion advertisements, or art. The real body is lumpy, spotty, hairy, blotchy, uneven, and rounded, and can be seen in almost every color, height, width, and age. It can be hard to look at a real person posing in an art studio and know where to begin. Artists use techniques for drawing the nude model (called "life drawing") that allow you to see the structure of the body, no matter how hidden. Once you have eyes to see it, you will find that every person's body is beautiful. Beauty is not a subject matter; it resides in the eyes and mind of the artist.

The Greek philosopher Epictetus advised, "One of the best ways to elevate your character immediately is to find worthy role models to emulate…There is nothing false in this. We all carry the seeds of greatness within us, but need an image as a point of focus in order that they may sprout." This is true in life and art. By studying great drawings done by historical and contemporary masters, you learn at the source, from the artists themselves, what makes a great drawing.

You deserve every tool for self-expression. This is your art, your tradition, your time. Take your voice and add it to the tradition as if the history of art has saved the best for now.

Before we begin

Here are a few tips to keep in mind as you work through this book:

- **Develop your drawings lightly.** A light line erases easily without damaging the paper and allows you to go darker as your confidence increases. On an extra scrap of paper (outside the book), practice making a range of marks with your pencil. Start lightly, the pencil barely touching the paper, then press down firmly to make deep, rich darks. You can even get tracing paper or vellum to lay over the drawings and practice on before drawing in your book.

- **Take it slow.** Don't worry about trying to finish a drawing in one sitting. Accuracy and improving your eye will come with time.

- **Mark your boundaries.** To copy a full-page master drawing, make your drawing the same size as the one you are copying. As we start drawing, our picture may accidentally grow, pushing the heads and feet off the page. To prevent this, lightly draw lines from the top and bottom of the master drawing onto the blank page. This establishes the height of your figure. To determine the width of your figure, measure the original drawing with your pencil, ruler, or a scrap of paper, then mark that same width on the blank paper. It will be easier to correct your drawing if it is exactly the same size as the one you are copying, because you can flick your eyes back and forth between the images to scan for differences.

- **Check for accuracy.** While I recommend freehand drawing, it's okay to find anchor points, such as the halfway point of the figure, or head lengths. If your drawing is the same size as the master drawing, you can measure directly from the original drawing to check if your heights are correct by placing a T-square (or a piece of paper) across both your drawing and the original to see if they align as you lower your T-square down the figure. However, try freehand drawing first before using measurements to double-check accuracy.

Materials

The only materials you need for this book are a good pencil, an eraser, and a pencil sharpener. For drawings with color, you can use colored pencils in sepia or umber.

I prefer to start with a hard graphite pencil, such as an F (or H), to keep the first lines light, before switching to a softer pencil to get darker. When buying a pencil at the art store, look at the stamp at the end of the pencil. "H" stands for "hardness" and "B" for "blackness"; the higher the number, the harder (and lighter) or softer (and darker) it is. I like to have a range from 2H to 2B. Mechanical pencils are also a good choice—even the inexpensive ones found in office supply stores—as they make a thin line and don't need to be sharpened. If you live near an art store you can get a better-quality pencil, but any pencil can be used, even the classic yellow schoolhouse #2 (which translates to an HB).

The pink erasers on the ends of pencils often leave damaging marks on the page. Instead, use a good white polymer eraser or a kneaded eraser.

Remember, you don't have to do an exact copy for the practice to have value; you can use a different medium or go lighter or darker. Many works in this book were created in charcoal or sepia Conté crayon or pencil, but can be copied in graphite. Charcoal is not recommended because it will smear on a smooth surface as it brushes against the opposite page.

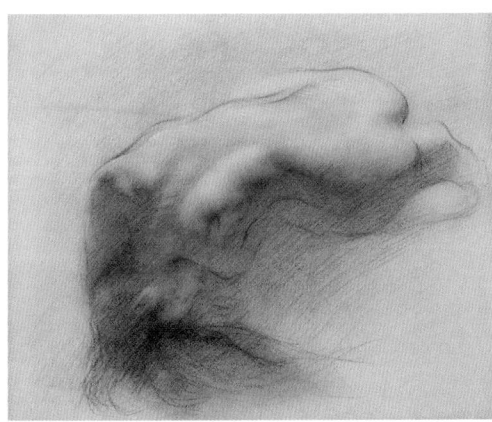

Juliette Aristides, *Figure Sketch*, 2014,
Stabilo pencil on glass, 10 x 12 inches
(25.4 x 30.5 cm)

A key to approaching the figure

This book builds sequentially, from beginning lines to rendering light and shade, helping you understand the drawing process from start to finish. We always work from general to specific, moving from large lines, shapes, and tones to smaller ones.

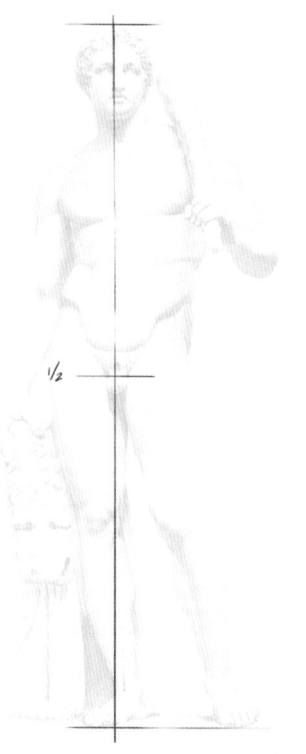

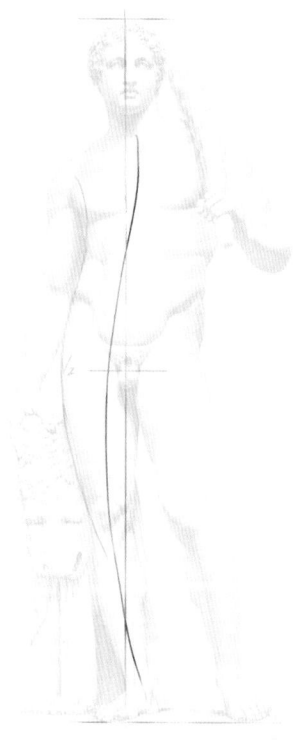

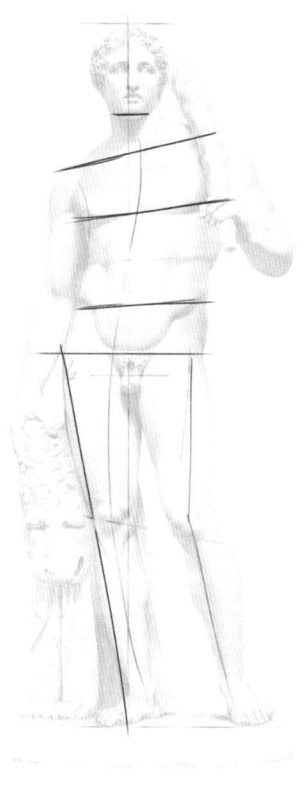

1. **Place the figure on the page**. Mark the top, bottom, and halfway point of your figure, followed by a centerline. This simple scaffolding determines the size of your figure and its placement on the page.

2. **Find the line of action**. Find a line of movement, from top to bottom, that carries your eye through the figure. This important stage cultivates your artistic vision and helps convey it to the viewer.

3. **Find tips and tilts.** Look across the figure to determine the tip and tilt of the shoulders, the nipples, the hip bones, and the pelvis. You can also determine which is the weight-bearing leg. These lines form an armature upon which to build your figure.

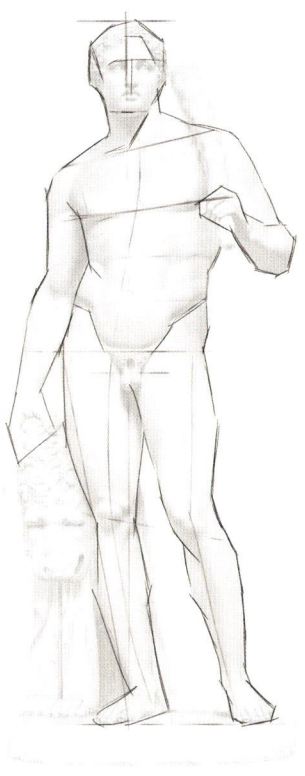

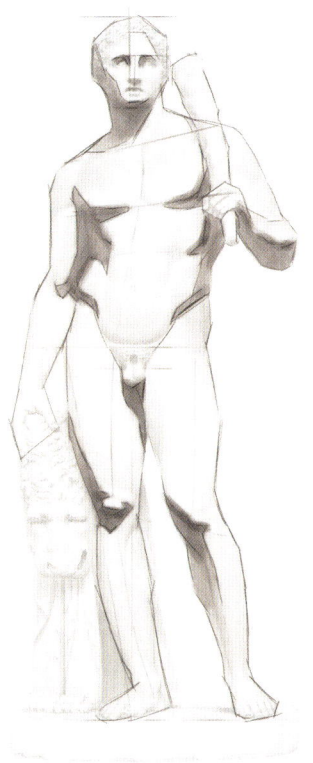

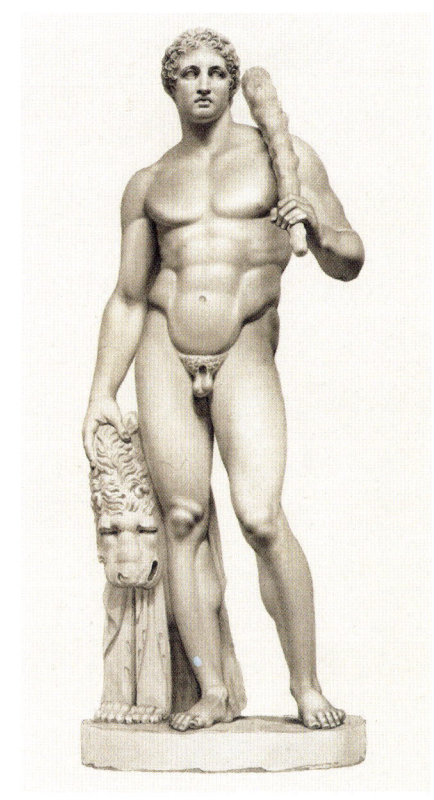

4. **Block in the figure**. Use straight lines to capture the angles of the body and the larger shadow shapes. Focus on the larger line directions rather than the nuanced contours.

5. **Map the shadows**. Separate the light from the shadows, flattening areas of the body into simple shapes and then lightly tone them.

6. **Add form.** Lay in halftones to create gradations of light across the surface of your figure, giving it the illusion of three dimensions.

John Samuel Agar, *Marquis of Lansdown Herakles,* 1806–35, ink and wash drawing, 15 ½ x 11 ⅘ inches (39.5 x 30 cm), J. Paul Getty Museum

Figure drawing demonstration

Most artists follow a more general progression, less exact than the steps on pages 12–13. In this drawing sequence, notice the flow from large lines to small forms. Each stage is an important step leading the artist to a beautiful drawing.

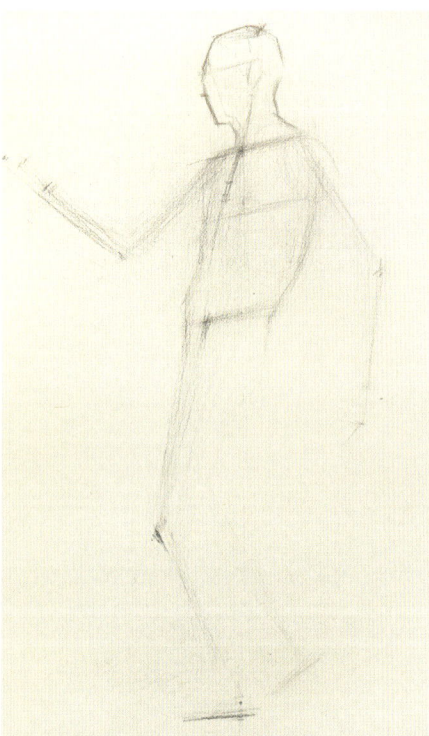

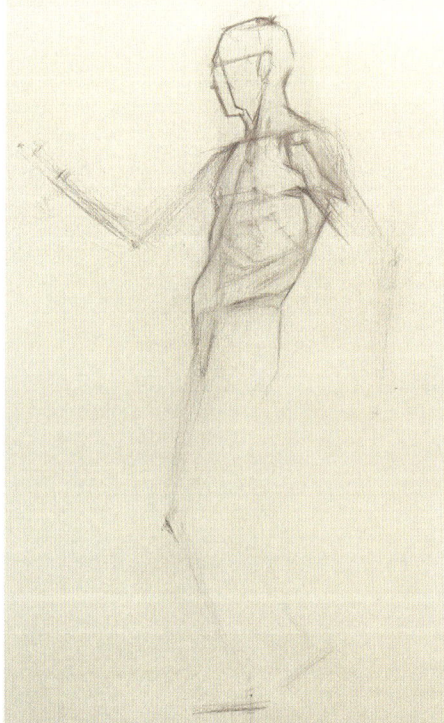

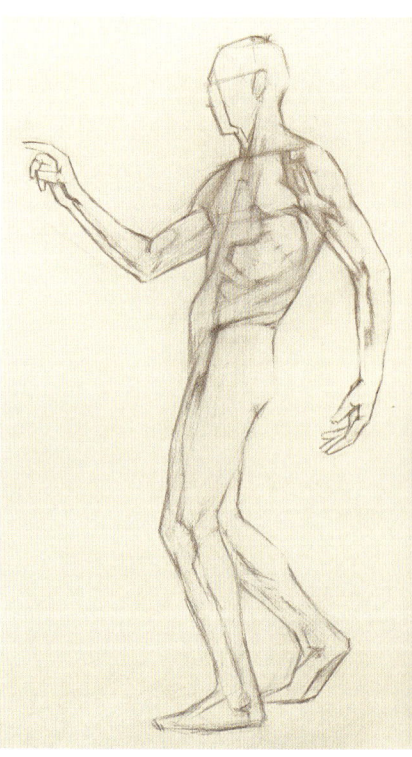

1. **Place the figure on the page**. The artist marked the top and bottom of the figure. A diagonal runs from the center of the neck and down the leg. Repeating angles are found: the line of the shoulders is the same as that of the hips and the top of the head. This is the armature of the figure.

2. **Block in the main masses.** The head, ribcage, and pelvis are placed. We notice that we are seeing a three-quarter view of the chest and a profile of the head. The artist jumped ahead to find some shadow shapes to structure the ribcage.

3. **Block in the figure.** The rest of the figure is blocked in. The shadow shapes are treated as an essential part of the figure; they are specific and well observed. Notice how the lines are kept angular and light, making them easier to work into later.

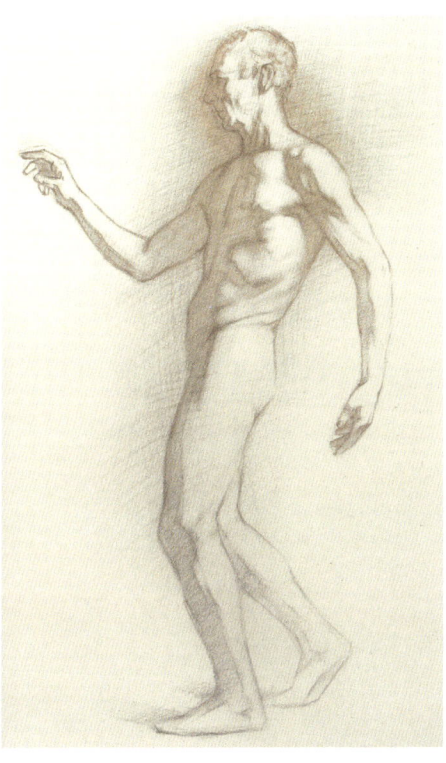 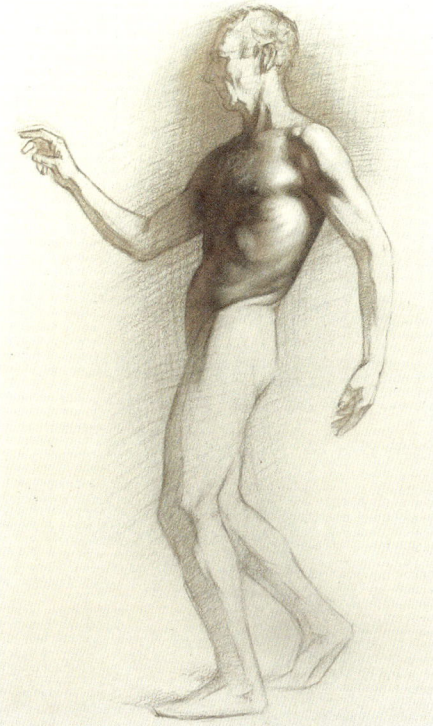 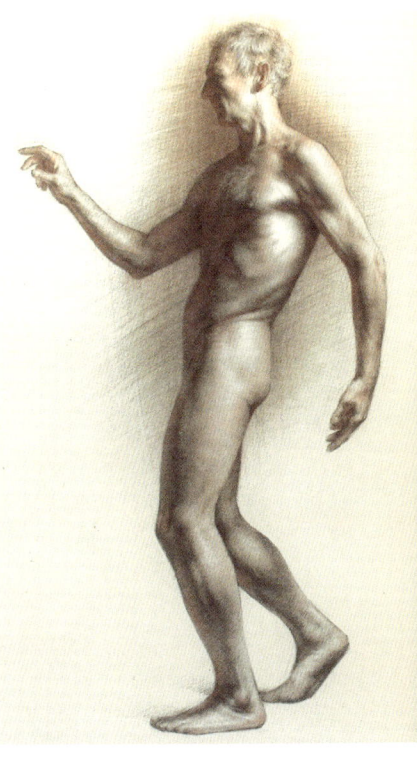

4. **Map the shadows**. Once the shadow shapes are drawn and shaded, the tones look like the continents on a map. There is now a clear separation between light and dark. Notice how our eye is drawn to the nuanced "coastlines" or edges of the shadow.

5. **Add form.** The shadow shape is darkened and a gentle gradation, or wash, of tone describes the surface of the skin and brings our attention to the lights. Placing these halftones adds dimension.

6. **Finish rendering form.** To finish the piece, the same kind of focused attention brought to the chest is applied to each part of the figure. Looking at small sections of the body in turn helps us capture the unique, personal aspects of our model.

Tenaya Sims, *Holger* (detail), 2011, pastel pencil on paper, 19 x 13 inches (48.3 x 33 cm)

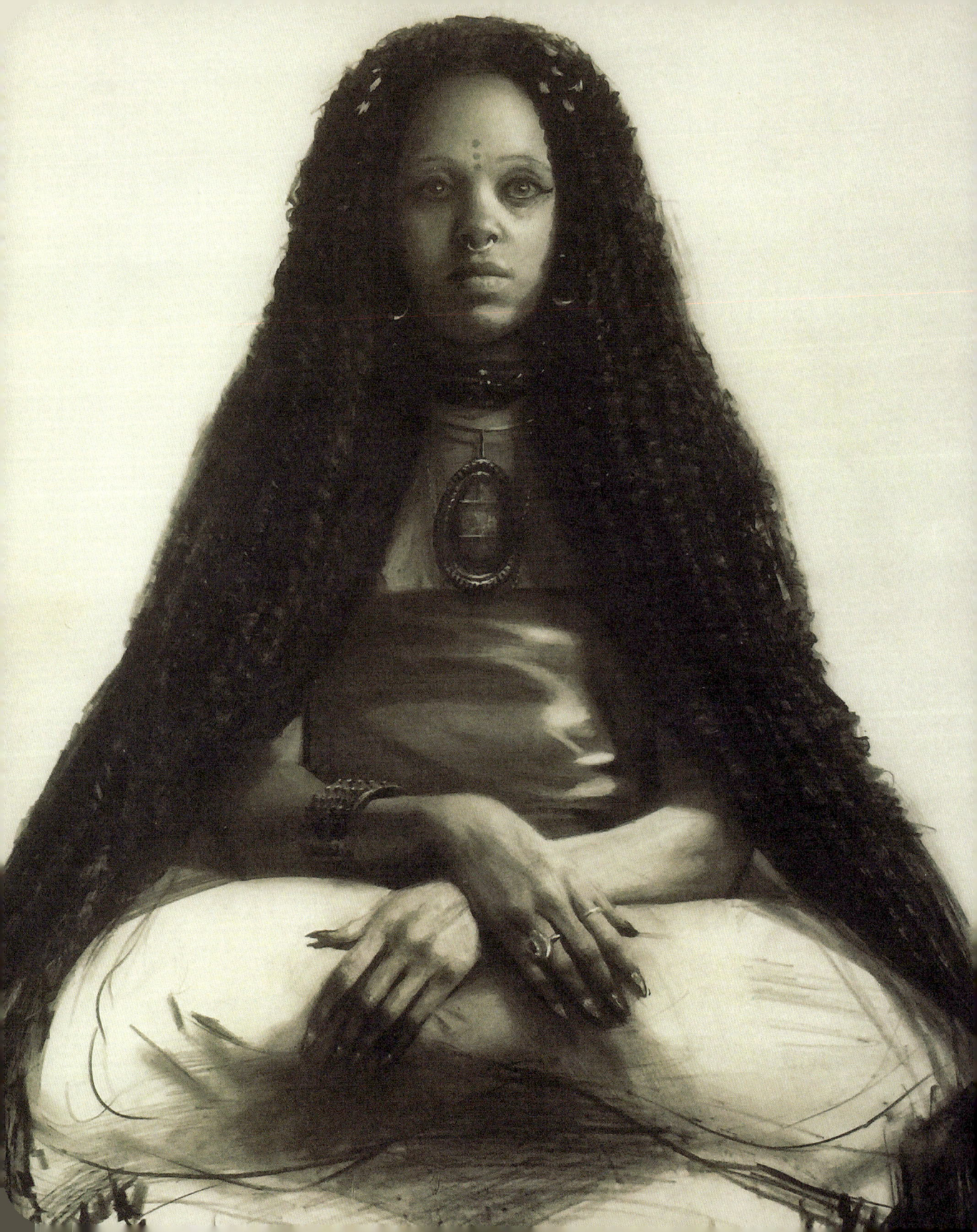

ONE

THE LINE OF ACTION

The framework of a work of art is also its most secret and deepest poetry.
—JAQUES VILLON

The lines we draw, just like our friends, have personalities: some are serious and analytical, while others are outgoing and emotional. The straight line and the curve provide us with different modes of expression, and good drawing allows them to work together. The straight line is rational, embodying intellectual uprightness. We think of the "plumb line of truth," a pillar of the community, the straight and narrow path. The straight line is man-made, constructed, and measurable; it expresses reason. By contrast, the curve is natural, emotional, and unpredictable, a line of feeling rather than thinking. We use words and expressions like "spiral out of control," "loopy," "shifting," "a whirlwind of energy." You would bring the curved line to a party and bring the straight line to negotiate your contracts.

In the straight-line family, each line direction has a unique symbolism. A vertical line is a tower pointing skyward, denoting strength, dignity, and balance. Action is required to see it: we must raise and lower our gaze. Meanwhile, the horizontal sleeps, it does not fight gravity but lays upon the earth with its full weight. The diagonal line is like a skier in action. It is in motion, dynamic, teetering on imbalance, running rather than resting or standing upright. It communicates action and movement.

None of us are intellectual *or* intuitive, emotional *or* logical. We are all of these qualities in varying degrees. The straight line needs the tempering of the curve to avoid being coldly mechanical; the curve needs the strength of the straight line or it becomes sloppy and superficial. The perfect balance of the two creates powerful art. How you use these lines, repeat them, and emphasize them becomes the rhythm and beat of your drawing, reinforcing your vision.

OPPOSITE: Steven Assael, *Portrait of Reign*, 2017, crayon and graphite on clay paper, 13 ½ x 11 ½ inches (34.3 x 29.2 cm), Kalamazoo Art Institute, Michigan

Seeing the line of action

When I lived in New York City, I took chess lessons from a speed chess player in Washington Square Park. My teacher always reminded me not to move a piece without knowing why. It sounds easy, but it isn't when the clock is ticking. The same is true in drawing. Before making your first mark, take a moment or two to study the model and find what inspires you. At first you may not see anything. Then gradually, as you would see faces in clouds, connections and relationships emerge. Are there lines that sweep, like a compass swing, from the hairline into the neck before disappearing into the front of the chest? Does the model throw her shoulders back, making her look like the figurehead of a ship? Is there a diagonal starting at his back leg and ending at the back of his neck, as if he is about to leap? These beginning *lines of action* create a design that will still be evident in the finished drawing.

Attending my first life-drawing class, I thought the goal of drawing was simply accuracy. So, it came as a surprise when, while I was working carefully on a portion of the face, my instructor recommended placing a few strong line directions to capture the whole pose. Like a preview of a movie or a plot summary for a book, simple lines of action reveal the essential movements of the model. They enable us to draw with freedom based on what inspires us, rather than just copying what we see. They also teach us how to avoid incidental elements that cloud our vision and result in literal but lifeless drawings.

When starting a drawing, place on the page the fewest lines necessary to convey the pose with accuracy. We seek to account for as much of the body as possible in a single line, so a line that tracks from the head to the feet is more valuable than a short one from the head to the neck. The goal is simplicity, unity, and observed truth. Capturing a strong line of action at the start of your drawing gives it life. You are the designer, so choose the line that feels most important to you. There is no right answer; numerous artists drawing the same model may find very different starting lines.

There is no such thing as pure objective observation. Your observation, to be interesting, i.e., to be significant, must be subjective.

—HENRY DAVID THOREAU

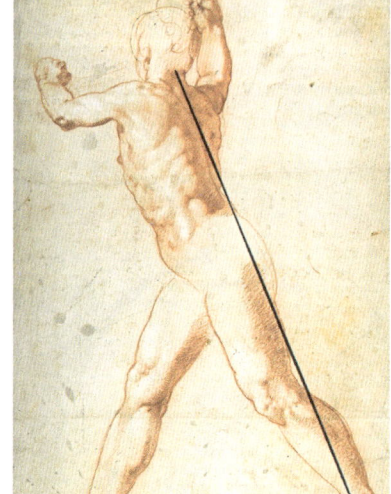

Notice how our eye travels from the back foot through to the head, as if the whole figure is resting along a diagonal.

Taddeo Zuccaro, *Standing Nude Man*, 1550, red chalk highlighted with traces of white gouache, 16 ⁹/₁₆ x 11 ⁵/₁₆ inches (42 x 28.7 cm), Metropolitan Museum of Art, New York

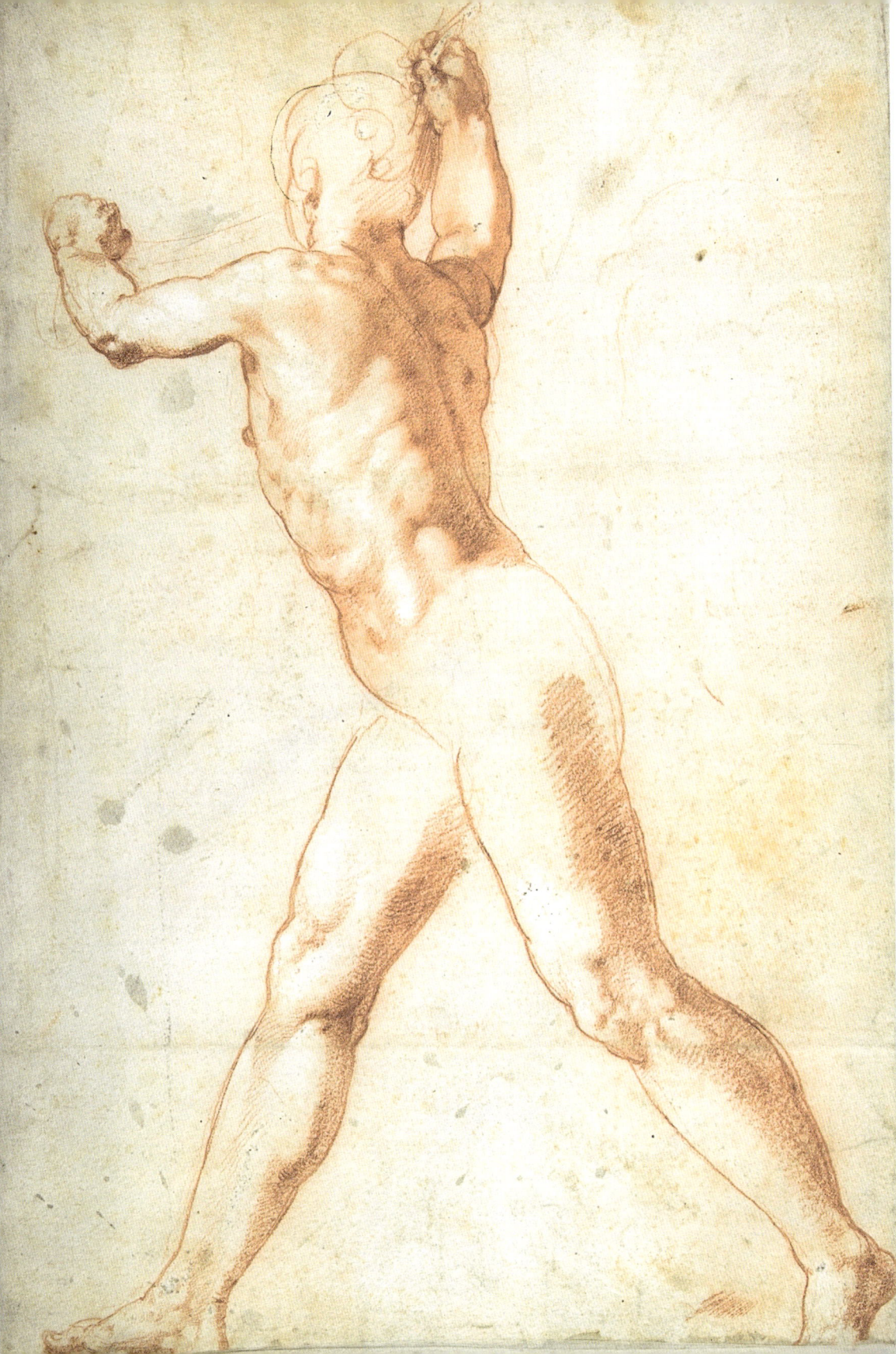

The diagonal

Diagonals show movement and direction, taking the eye from one area of the picture to another. In the space below, practice drawing strong diagonals. Then follow my example to find diagonal action lines in the drawing by Raphael, below, drawing them on the image. Finally, find the lines of movement in Rubens's *Anatomical Studies*, opposite. Try to keep your lines parallel, choosing only one or two line directions to study in each drawing.

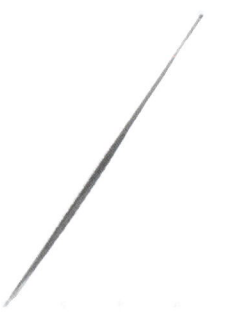

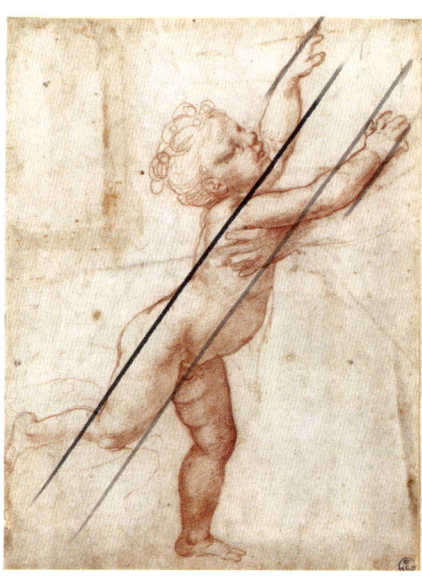

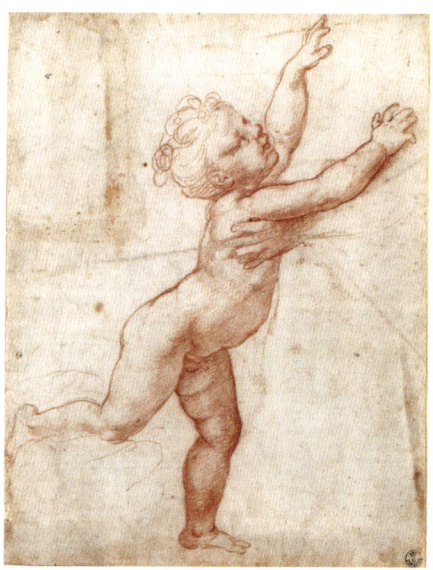

ABOVE: Raphael (Raffaello Sanzio), *Putto with Outstretched Arms*, date unknown, red chalk on white paper, 10 ⅝ x 8 ¼ inches (27 x 20.9 cm), Gabinetto dei Disegni e delle Stampe, Uffizi, Florence, Italy. Image courtesy of the Art Renewal Center

OPPOSITE: Peter Paul Rubens, *Anatomical Studies*, ca. 1600–5, pen and brown ink on paper, 11 x 7 ⅖ inches (27.9 x 18.7 cm), J. Paul Getty Museum

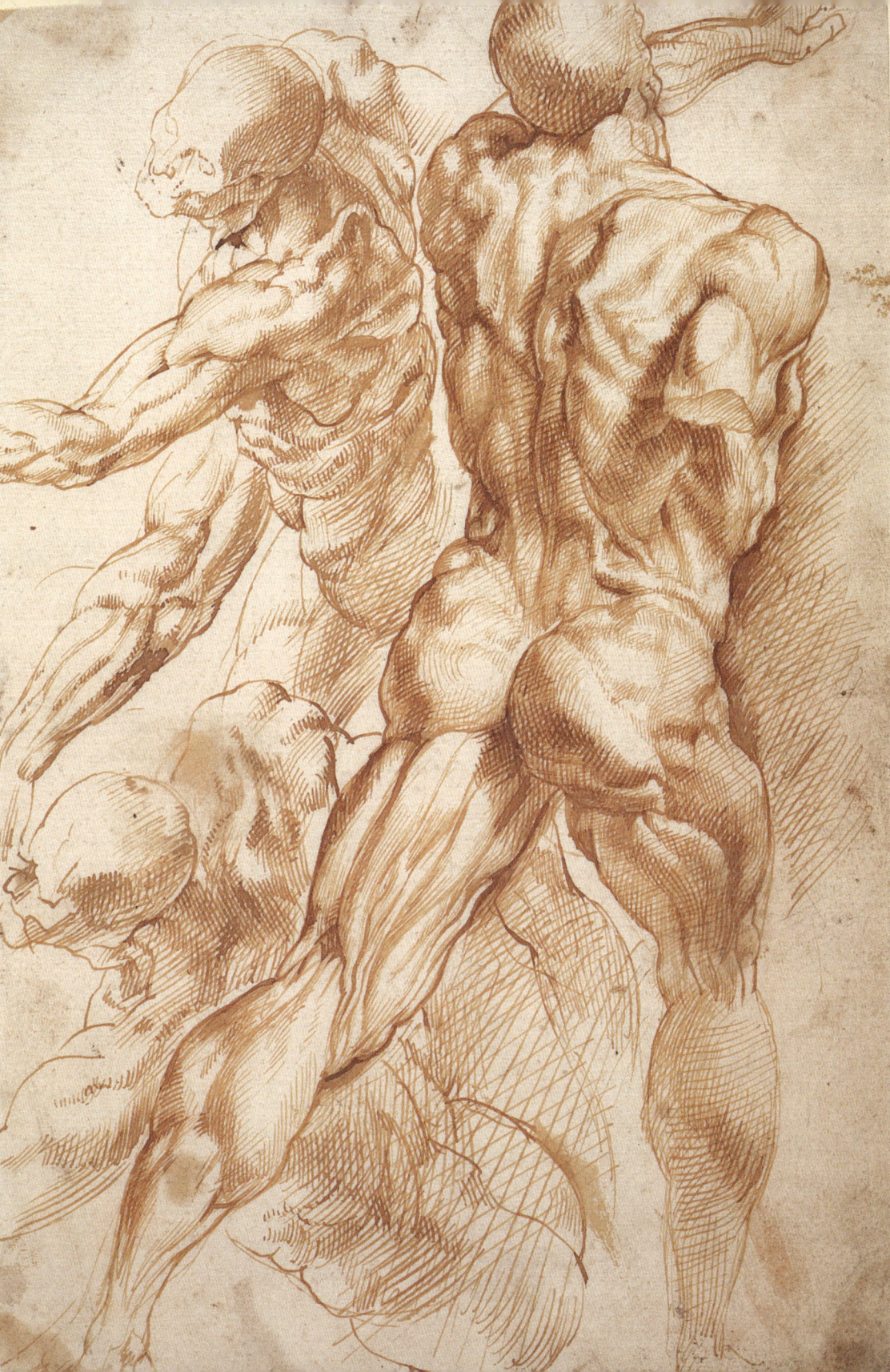

The arc

Curves are organic, fluid arcs that convey life and emotion. In Annibale Carracci's drawing, below, notice how the "C" curve of the body is echoed throughout the picture to emphasize the pose. It is a simple and powerful way to connect diverse parts of the picture: the head to the back, the arm to the waist. In the space below, practice drawing curved lines, lightly trace the curved lines of action on the Carracci piece. Finally, find the curves in the picture on the opposite page. See how many times you can find the curve repeated.

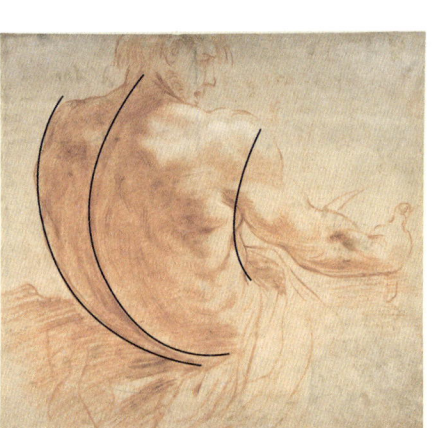

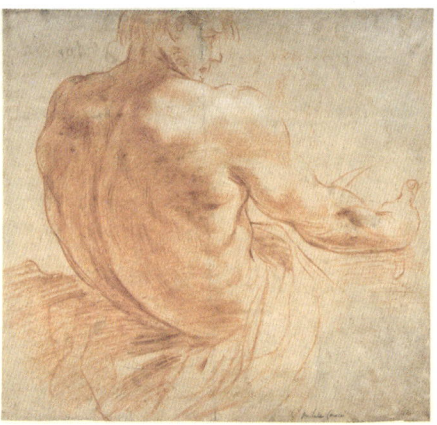

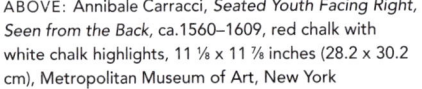

ABOVE: Annibale Carracci, *Seated Youth Facing Right, Seen from the Back*, ca.1560–1609, red chalk with white chalk highlights, 11 ⅛ x 11 ⅞ inches (28.2 x 30.2 cm), Metropolitan Museum of Art, New York

OPPOSITE: Marcel Sijben de Maroye (1878–1962), title and date unknown, red chalk on paper, size unknown, collection of Jordan Sokol and Amaya Gurpide

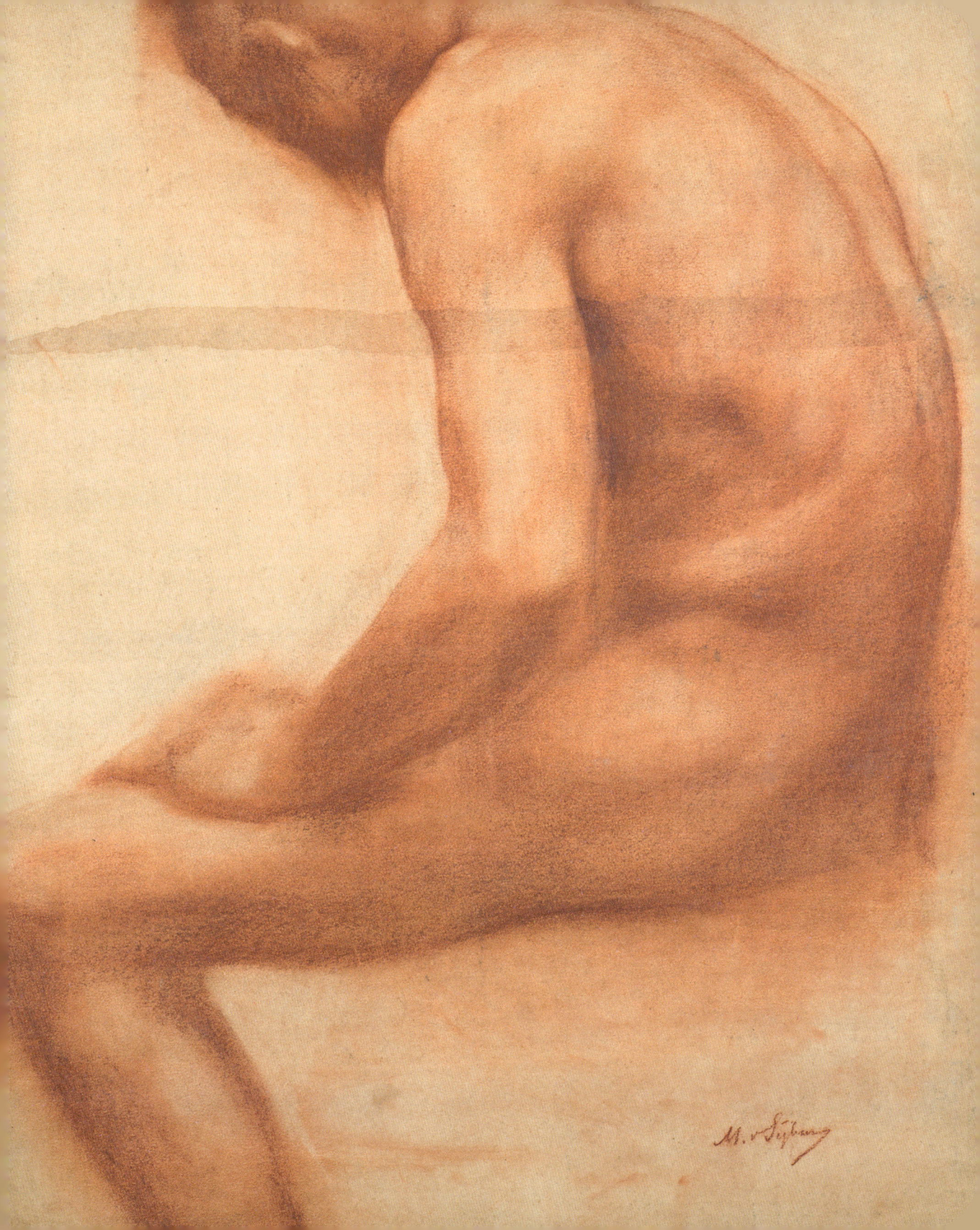

The "S" curve

A serpentine line, sometimes called the "line of beauty," captures the twisting, alternating motion of the reverse curves found in the body. This "S" curve leads your eye on a meandering path from one area of the figure to another. The curved line in Hendrick Goltzius's *Apollo*, below, is just one of the many ways a line can snake. Practice drawing S curves in the space below, then draw the S curve on Goltzius's work. Finally, find the serpentine line in the figure opposite, running from the head to the belly down through the leg.

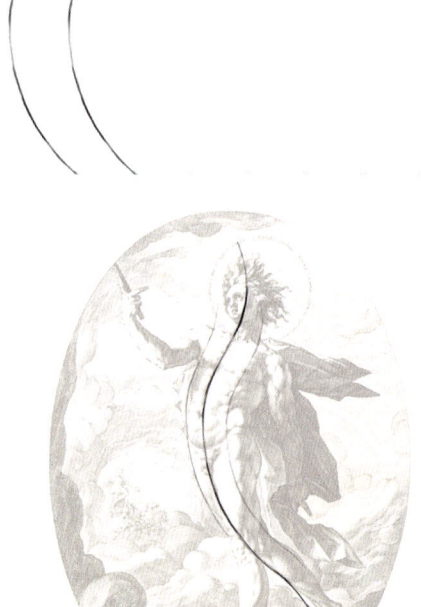

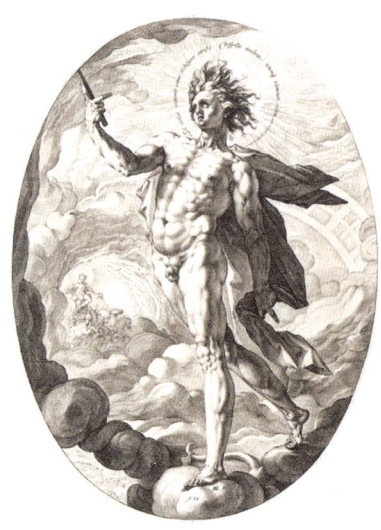

ABOVE: Hendrick Goltzius, *Apollo*, 1588, engraving, 13 ¾ x 10 ⅜ inches (34.9 x 26.4 cm), Metropolitan Museum of Art, New York (the Elisha Whittelsey Collection, the Elisha Whittelsey Fund, 1951)

OPPOSITE: Unknown French artist, untitled, late nineteenth century, charcoal on paper, 17 ½ x 12 inches (44.5 x 30.5 cm), collection of Jordan Sokol and Amaya Gurpide

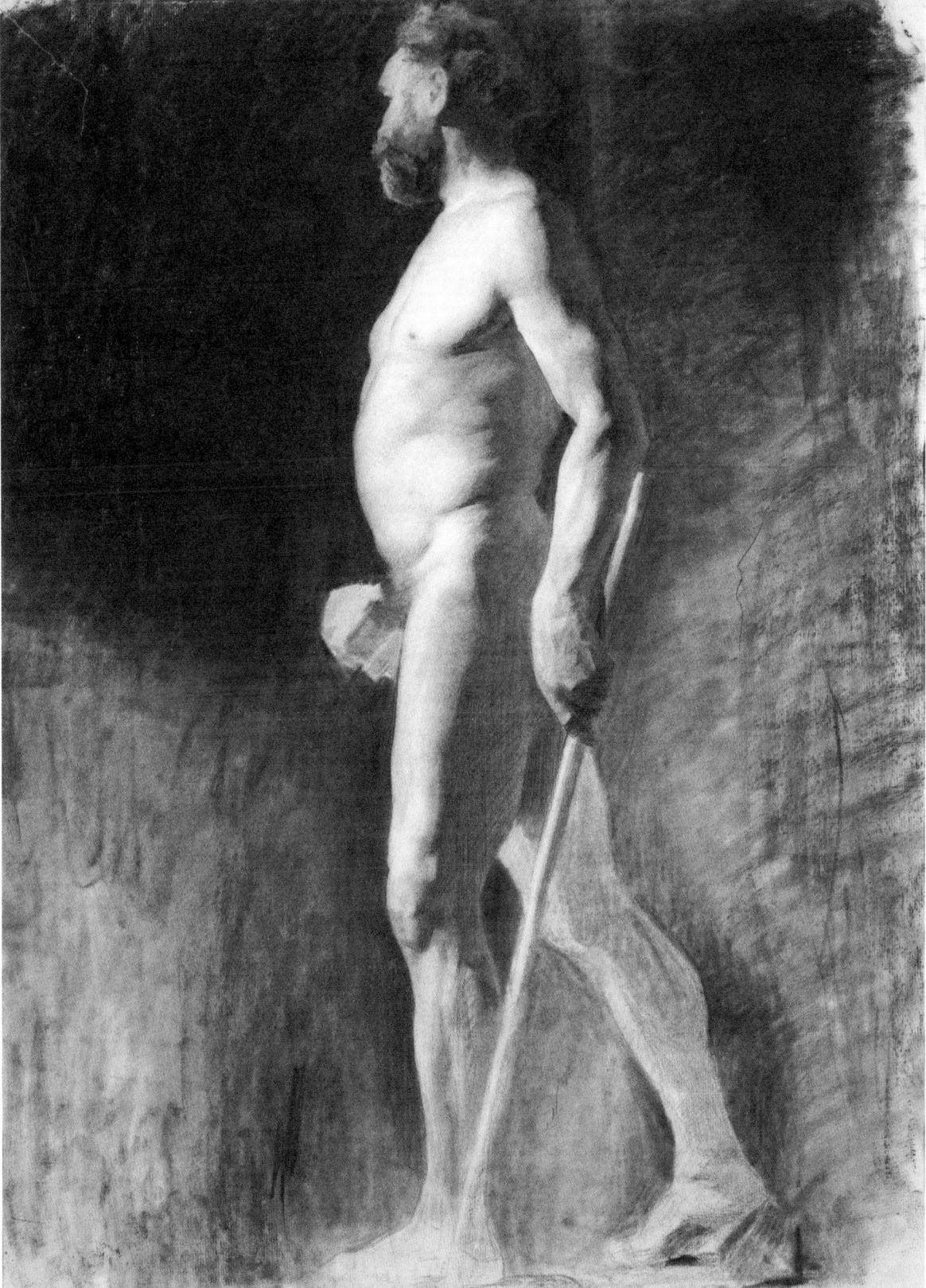

Lines of action

Find the repeating action lines in these drawings and sketch directly on the image below and on the faded, ghosted image on the opposite page. In *Sleep*, find the curve that flows from the feet to the head. On the opposite page, follow the line of the mountain as it leads to the arc on the wall. See it repeat as it flows from the man's feet and along the woman's body through the curve of her head. Can you see it anywhere else?

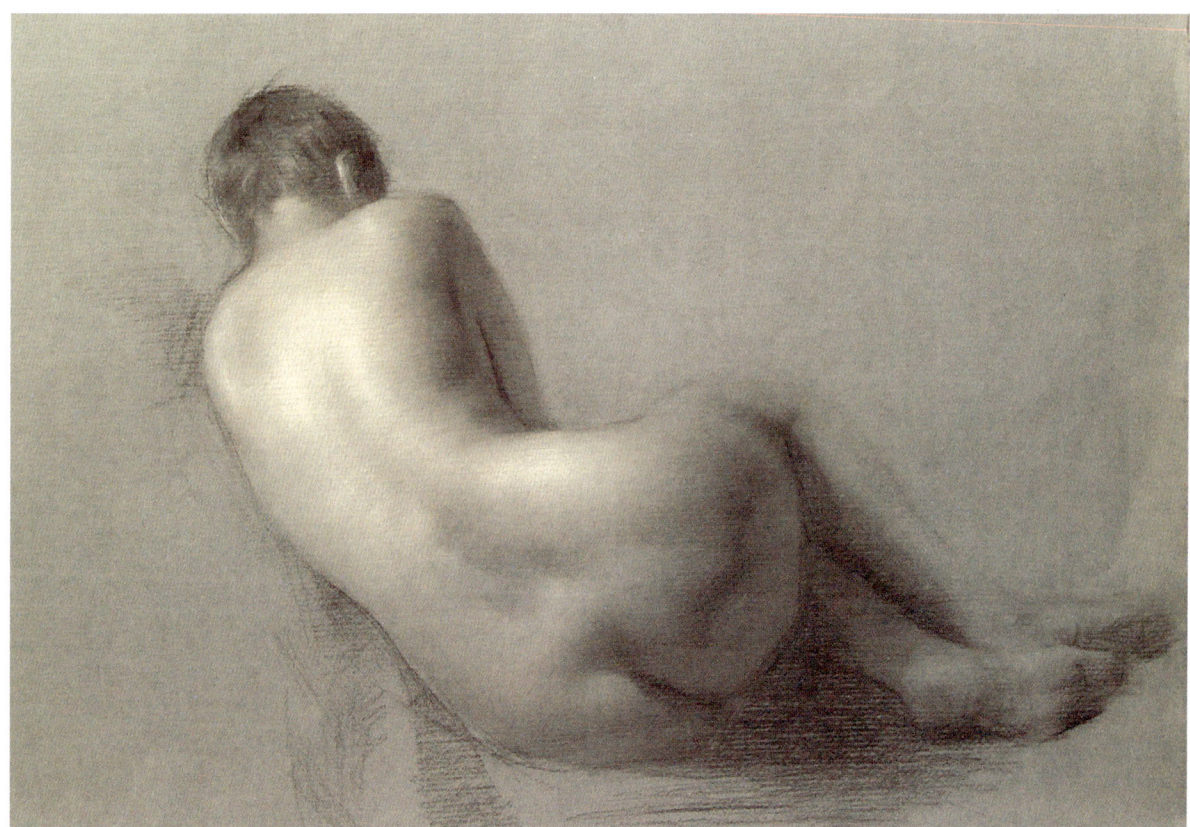

ABOVE: Juliette Aristides, *Sleep*, 2013, charcoal on toned paper heightened with white, 24 x 28 inches (61 x 71.1 cm)

OPPOSITE: Luigi Schiavonetti after William Blake, *The Soul Hovering over the Body, Reluctantly Parting with Life, from* The Grave, *a Poem by Robert Blair*, 1813, engraving, 6 ⅜ x 8 ¹⁵⁄₁₆ inches (16.2 x 22.7 cm), Metropolitan Museum of Art, New York (Harris Brisbane Dick Fund, 1917)

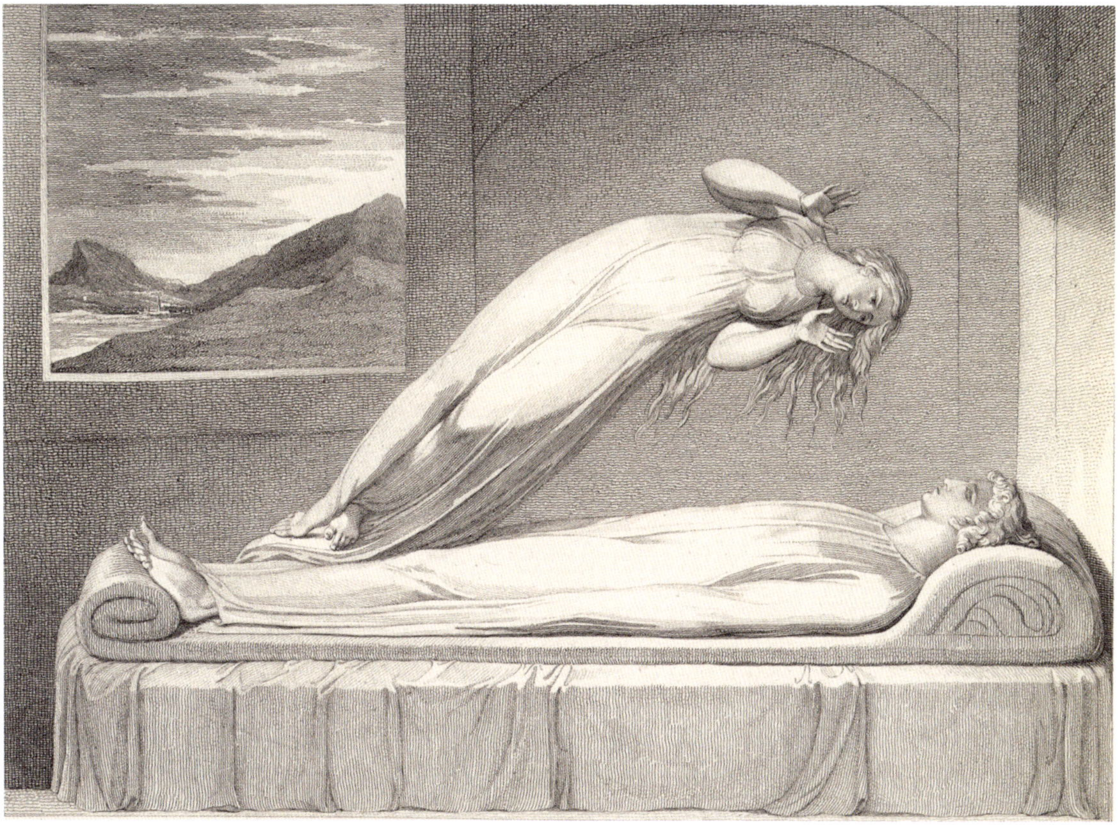

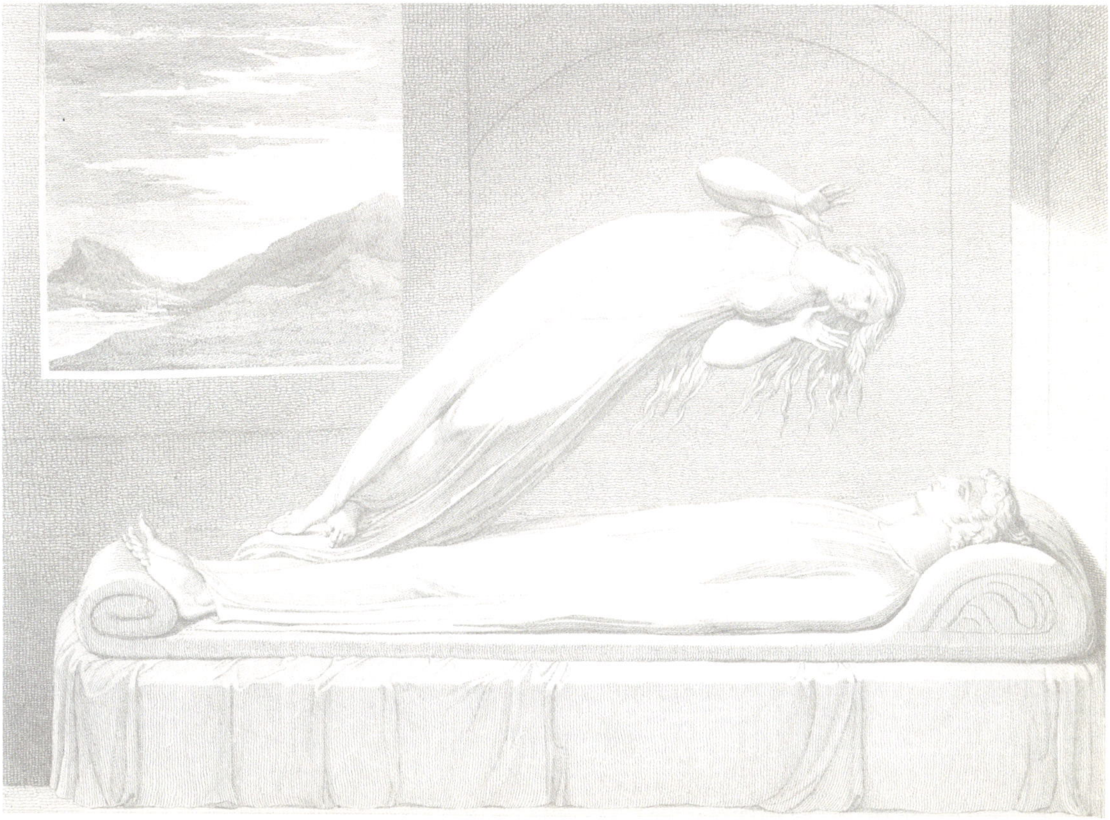

Gesture drawing

To see how the action lines inform the movement of these drawings, sketch over each figure on the opposite page. Start with an action line that describes the essence of the pose, then find the tips and tilts of the ribcage, head, and pelvis. Next, turn the page and freely sketch those gesture drawings in the space provided, focusing on the directional lines to create movement.

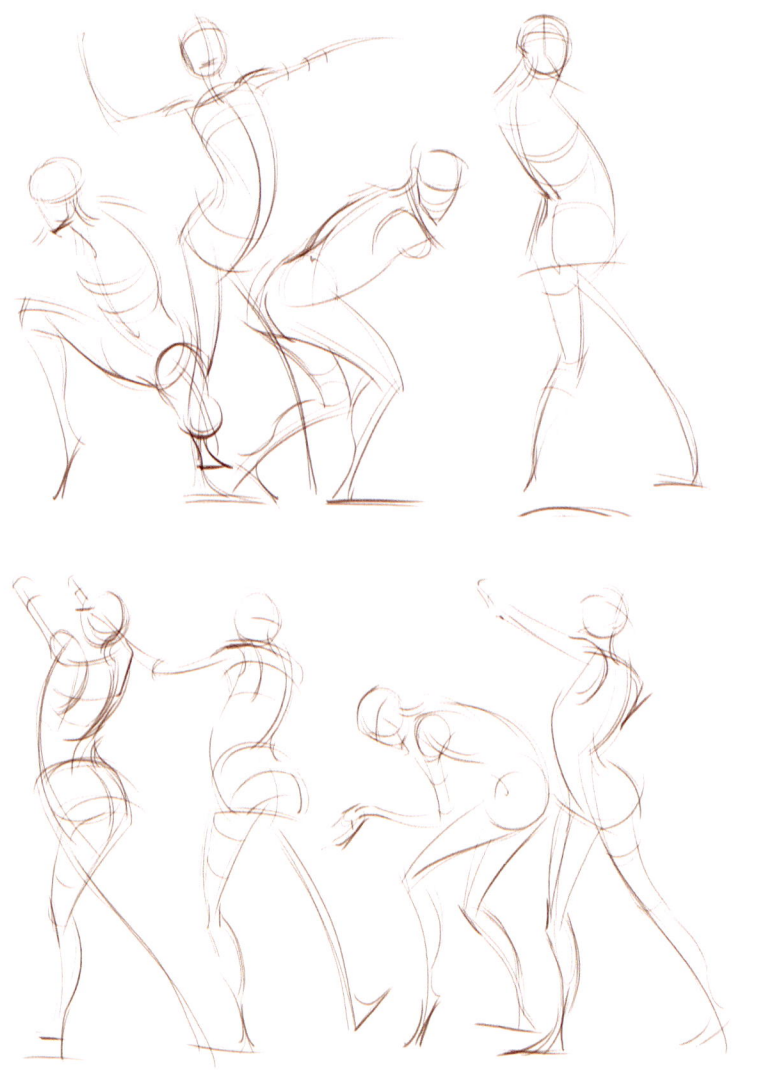

Michael Hampton, *Gestures* (detail), 2018, digital drawing

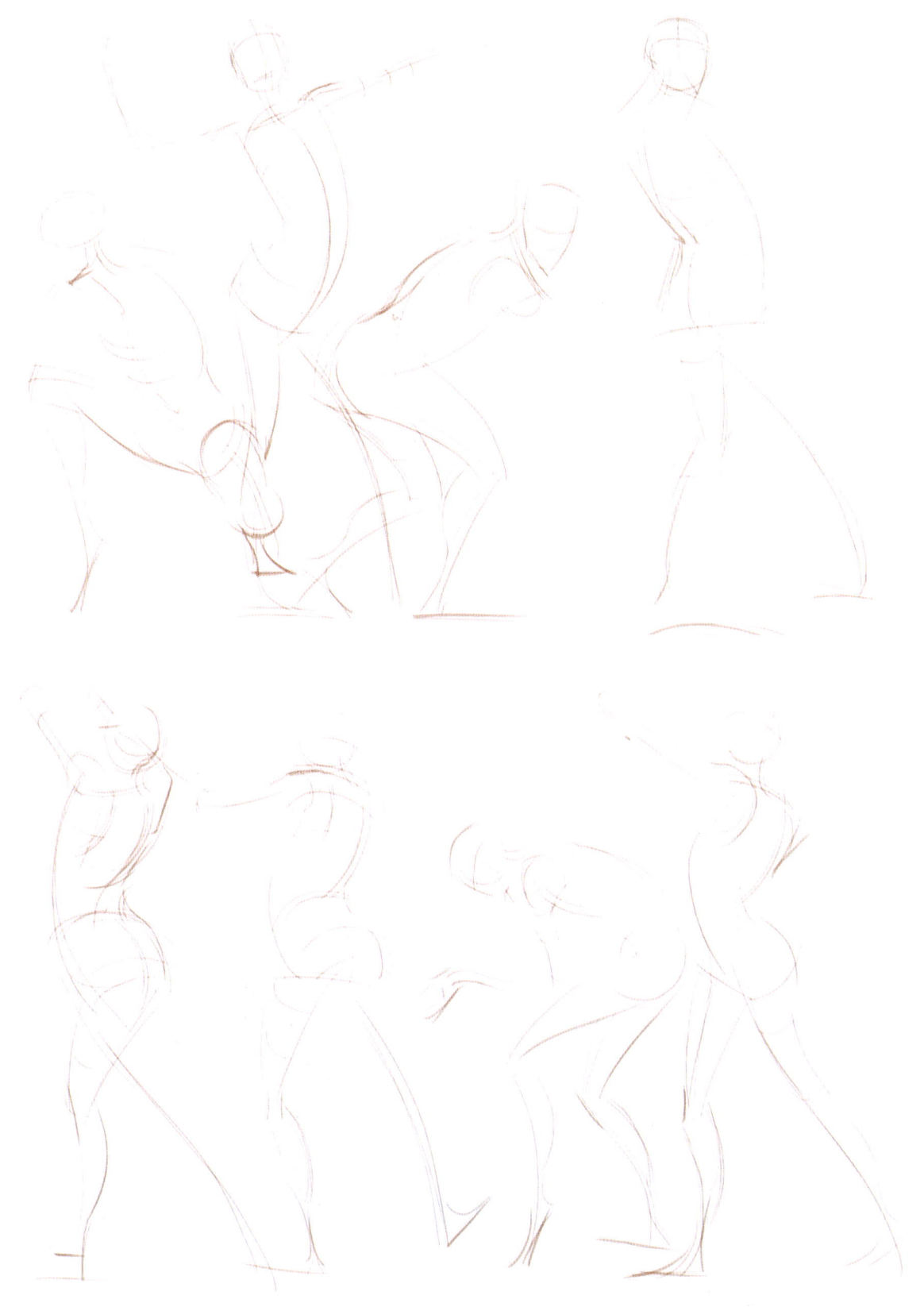

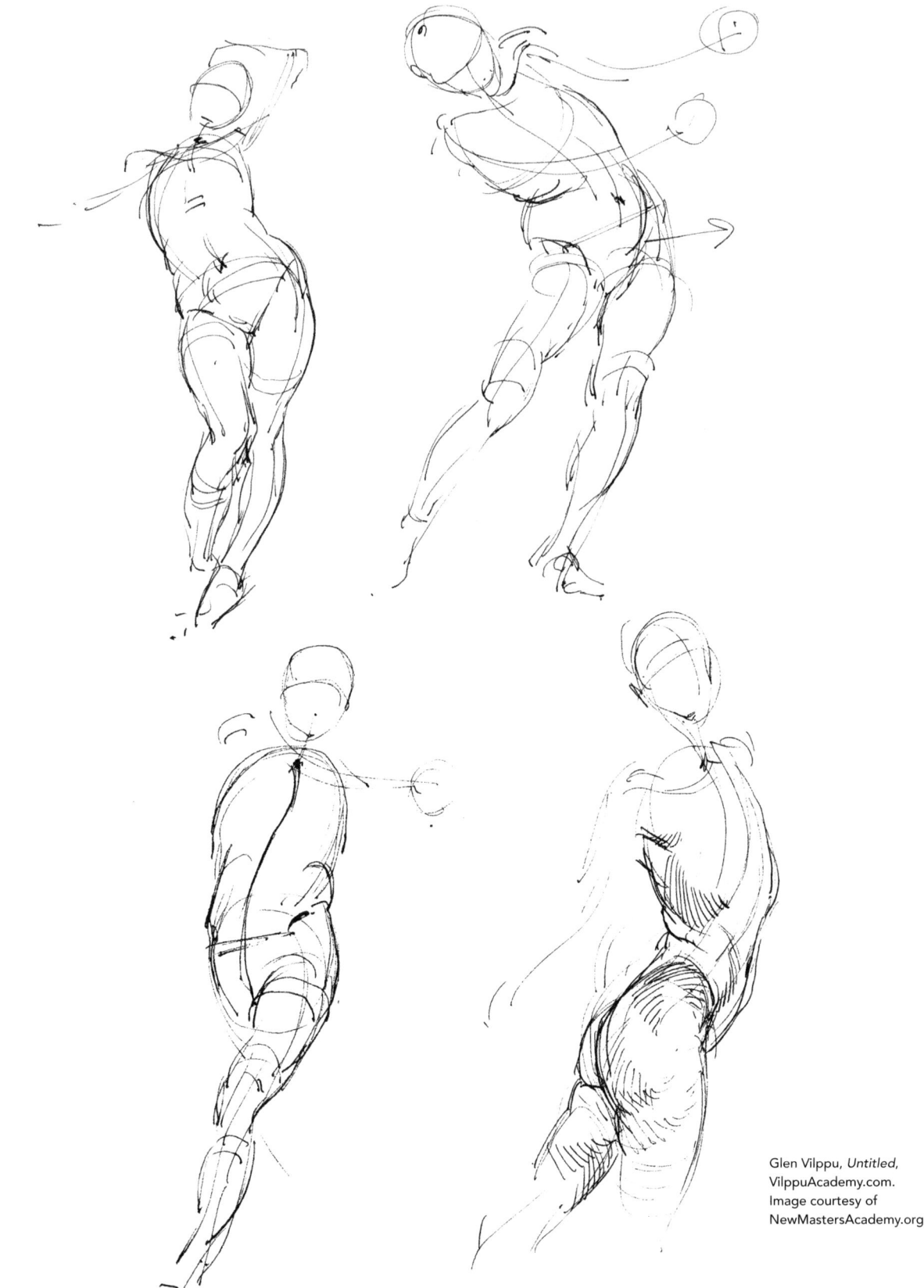

Glen Vilppu, *Untitled*,
VilppuAcademy.com.
Image courtesy of
NewMastersAcademy.org

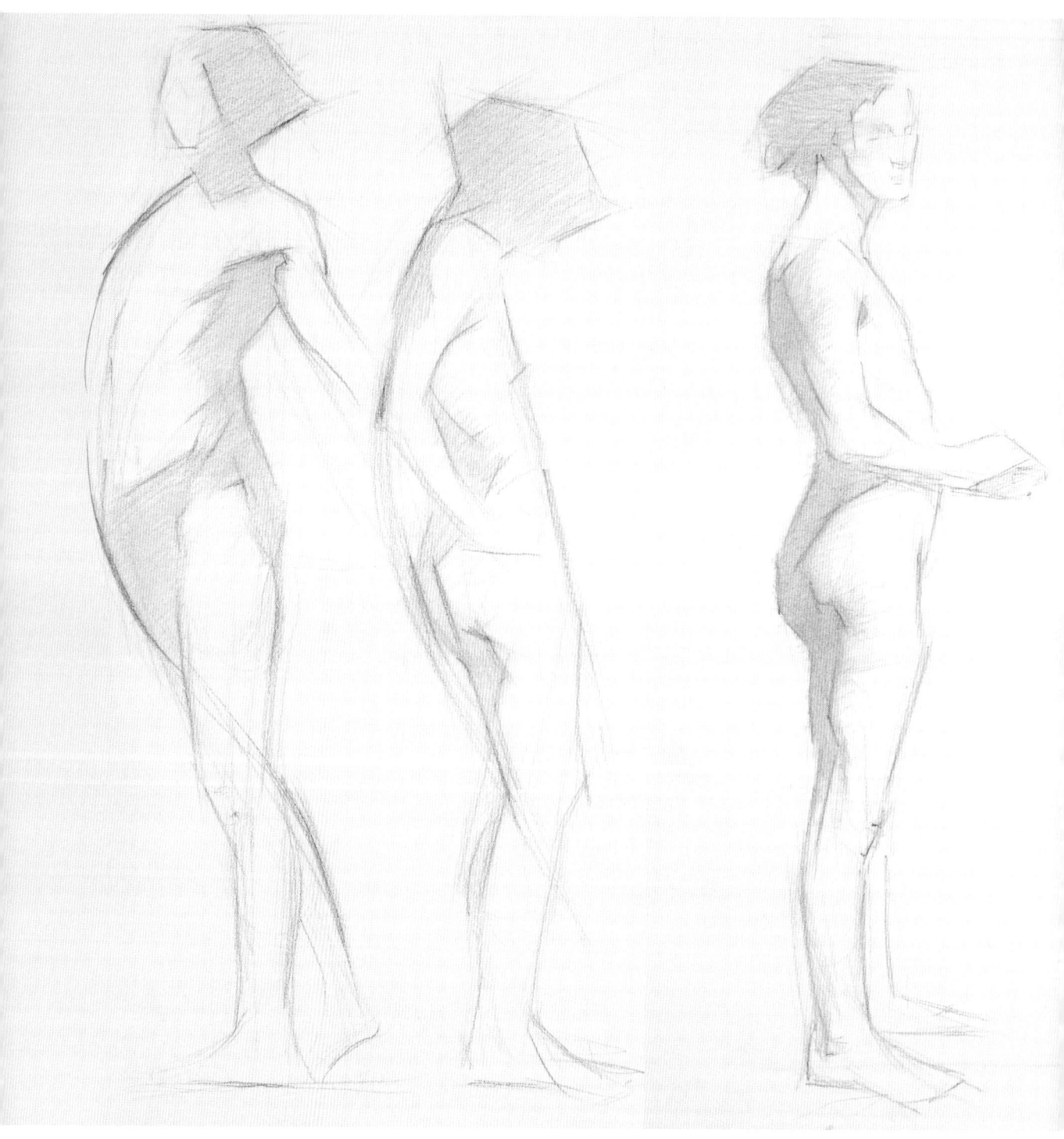

Juliette Aristides, *Five-Minute Gesture Drawings*, 2017, sepia pencil on paper, 18 x 18 inches (45.7 x 45.7 cm)

Sketch the figures in the space above. First, mark the placement of the head and feet. Then sketch the action line of each pose, noting later how these lines inform your finished sketches.

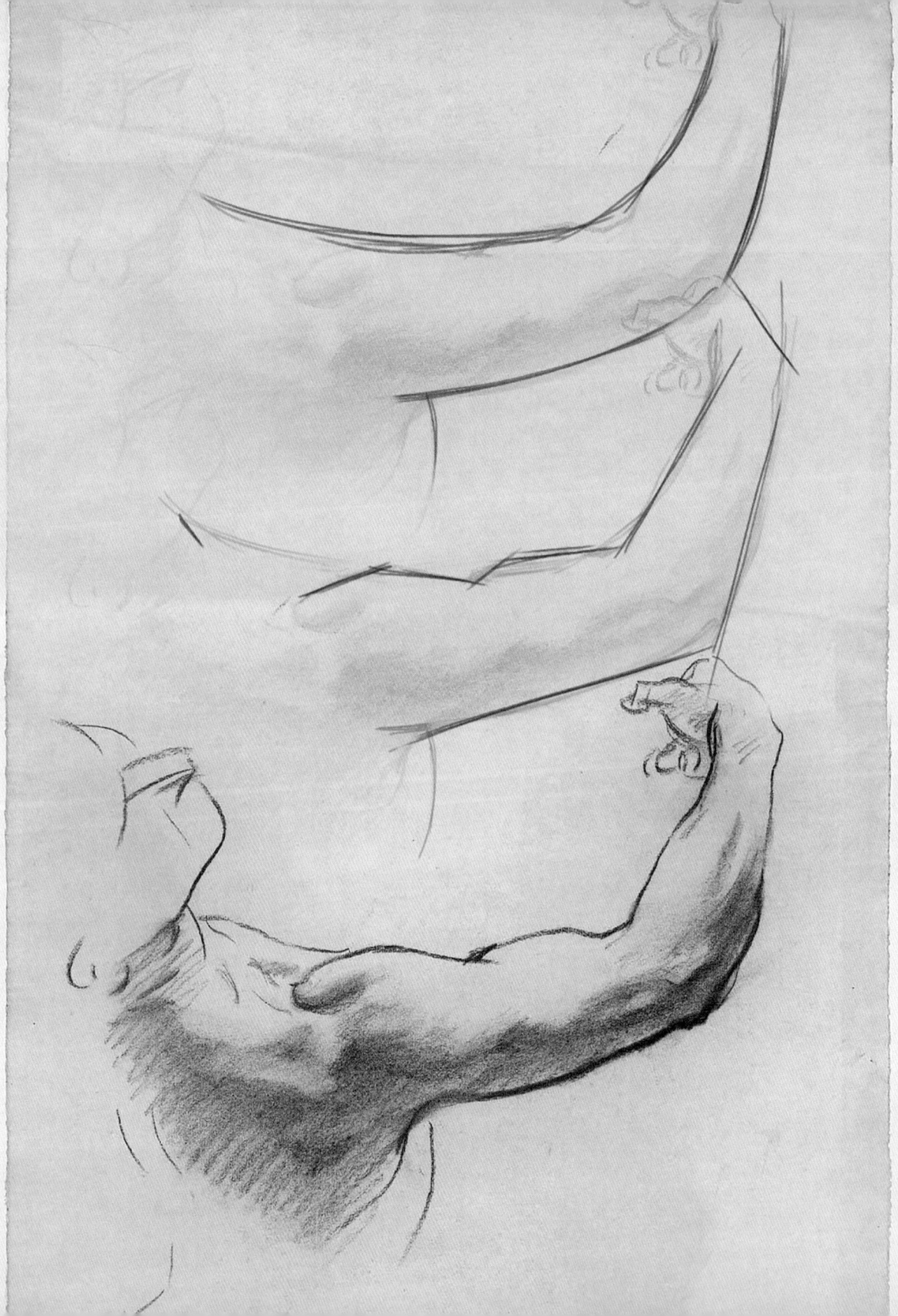

TWO

THE
BLOCK-IN

To start with a deep impression, the best, the most interesting, the deepest you can
have of the model; to preserve this vision throughout the work; to see nothing else;
to admit of no digression from it; choosing only from the model the signs of it.
—ROBERT HENRI, *THE ART SPIRIT*

A *block-in* is an abstract shape constructed with straight lines that captures your subject in a general, "blocky" way. If you invest the time to find the likeness of a pose using broad lines, without detail, in this early stage, you'll achieve greater accuracy in the final drawing.

The block-in approach to figure drawing can be thought of the way an architect designs a building: she starts by laying the framework, then works from large to small shapes, from general to specific. You may have only a few general directional or structural lines by the end of this first stage, but they should capture a likeness and the *feeling* of the pose. Aim for simplicity and resist the urge to put in a lot of small changes in the beginning. If the first five or six lines don't feel generally accurate, more lines will just make those mistakes harder to find.

In the analysis of John Singer Sargent's drawing of arms, opposite, the drawing at the top of the page shows the line of action: a sweeping curve. Below this is the block-in: the bones of a drawing, created with straight-line increments to capture the proportion and inflection of the arm. Lastly, Sargent's original drawing brings it all together: the movement of the curve, the control and precision of the block-in, and subtle rounding and modeling to capture the details seen in the life model.

OPPOSITE: Ovidio Cartagena's analysis of John Singer Sargent, *Sketch for Heaven*, 1903, charcoal on paper, dimensions unknown, Museum of Fine Arts, Boston

Blocking in the figure

The block-in uses straight lines to set the precise location and tip or tilt of the general angles of your figure drawing. Imagine I gave you a collection of toothpicks and asked you to place them on your paper in a way that captured the pose of a model. You would be able to get both accurate proportion and correct tips and tilts, yet no detail. That is the goal of this stage of the drawing. As the nineteenth-century artist Daniel Parkhurst wrote, "All good work is from the general to the particular, from the mass to the detail. Keep that in mind as a fundamental principle in good work, whatever the kind."

In chapter one, we studied the emotion conveyed by the action line. Now we turn our focus to the straight-line block-in to pursue accuracy and precision. Excellent drawing requires carefully considered relationships of all our lines. At the end of this stage, you will have something that looks like a wire armature with a simplified contour placed on top. This stage is critical to laying a solid foundation ensuring that your final drawing is correct.

Look at the image on page 38, showing a block-in line drawing on the left and the finished piece on the right. Can you see the lightly placed centerline that runs between the center of the shoulders and then down into the base? This line locks in the vertical alignment, the top over the bottom. Next, notice the lines horizontal securing the angle of the shoulders and the tips of the ribcage, hips, and under the buttocks. These few lines ensure that the left and right sides of the figure relate in a meaningful way and capture the movement of the pose. Finally, notice how the artist found the straight-line increments of the contour and shadow shapes.

To block in the armature of your figure, use simple straight lines to find your first angles. These beginning lines are efficient because you only need to get the general direction correct to ensure a strong start to your drawing. The first decision is to decide how big your drawing will be. *If you are copying a drawing in this book, try to make your drawing the same size as the one you are copying.*

Next, lightly draw a vertical line to show your figure's center of balance. Find the halfway point along the line and make a tick. On a standing figure, the halfway point is often at the bottom of the pelvic bone, near where the figure bends at the hips.

To find the angles that run horizontally across the body, use your pencil or a skewer or knitting needle to convert curves to straight lines. Use straight lines to indicate the tip of the

OPPOSITE: Analysis of Harold Speed's demonstration drawing from his classic book, *The Practice and Science of Drawing*

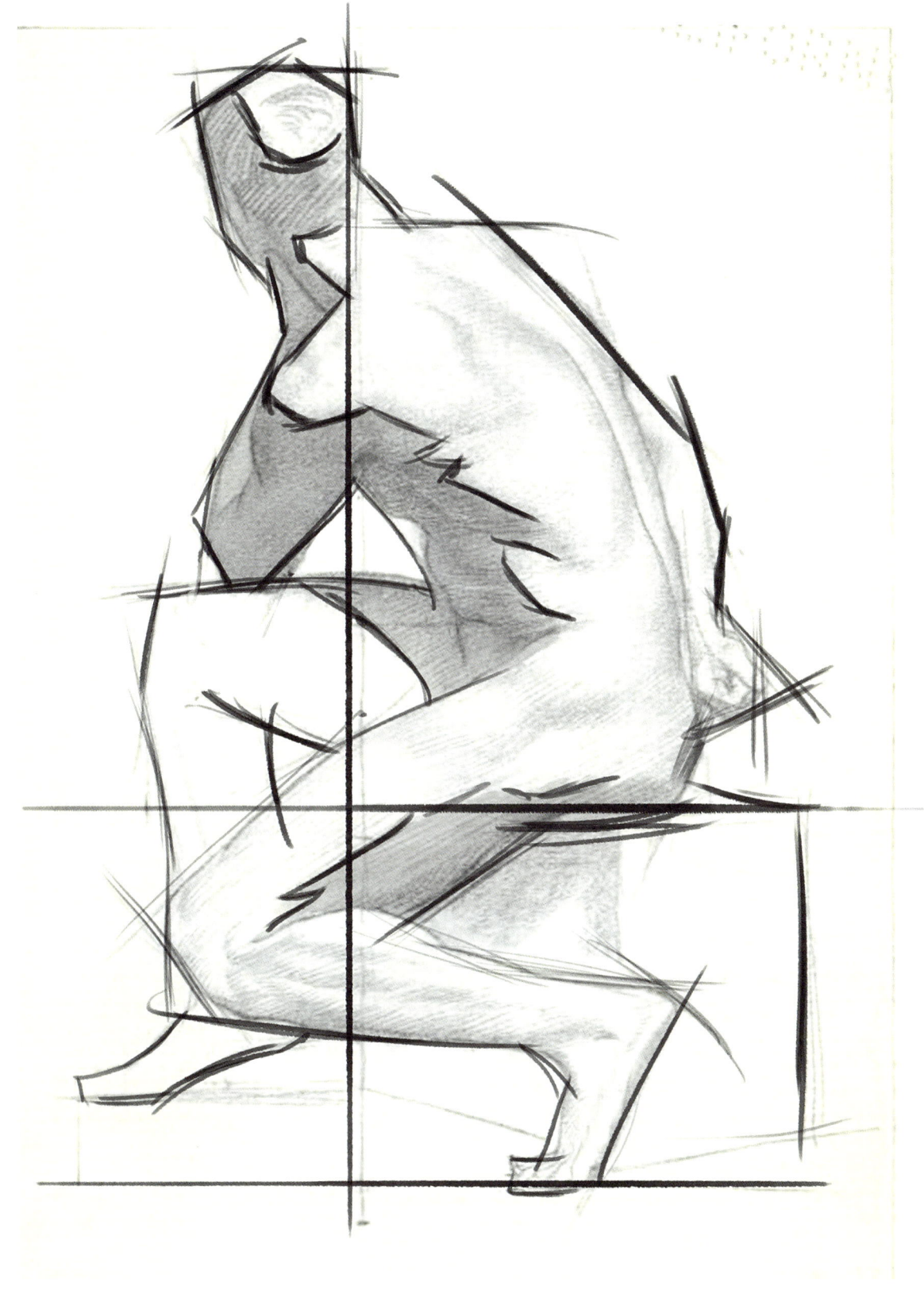

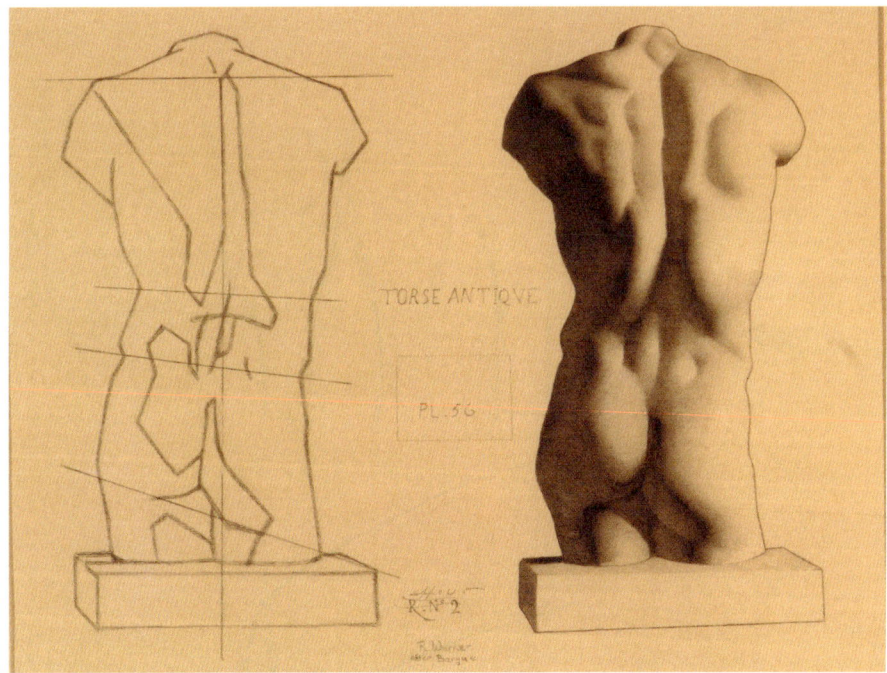

shoulders by running a line across the clavicles. Line up your skewer across the hip bones to see how the pelvis tips from the front, or across the sacrum from the back to find the angle of the hips. To determine the tilt of the head, find the centerline that runs along the nose to the chin in relation to the right-angle tip of the eyes. Finally, look for the weight-bearing lines of the legs.

When trying to identify a general line direction, look past all the tiny angles and incidental curves to find the average. Use your skewer to find the angles by lining it up along the big movements of the pose, then see in what direction your skewer is pointing. To block in the armature of your figure, locate its "bony landmarks," parts of the skeleton that lie just under the skin and aren't covered by thick layers of muscle, such as the collarbone and hip bones.

Once you've blocked in the masses above, find the large action lines of the figure, such as a line running from the legs to the side of the ribcage and the head. You might end up with just a few placement lines, or get a shape that looks like a kite, to create a simplified contour for a compact pose.

In the following stages, work from general to specific as you build the figure:

1. Find the top, bottom, and halfway point to place your figure on the page.

2. Find the general angle directions of the pose and gesture while also including the tips and tilts of the head, ribcage, and pelvis. Once you have placed a few of the largest lines, adjust them until they seem intuitively accurate, capturing the essence of your subject. (This is a felt, rather than measured, accuracy.)

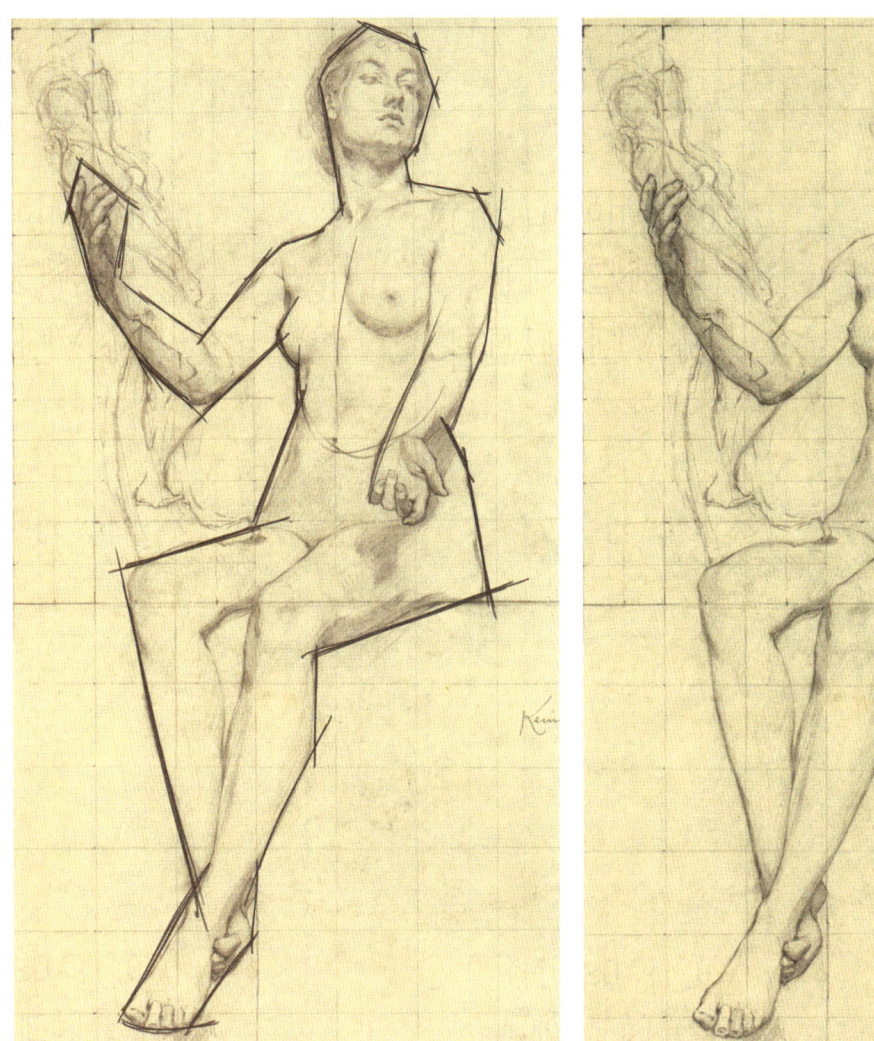

3. Site the largest angles of the body and find the outside or envelope shape.

4. With the scale, proportion, and gesture of the body established, you are free to find the smaller forms, knowing that the larger shapes are generally correct.

Over time, these stages will become intermingled. Your practice will feel fluid through experience and you will be able to alternate between capturing a simple gesture and the armature of the pose.

OPPOSITE: Robin Werner, *Copy after Charles Bargue Torso*, charcoal on paper, from *C. Bargue Cours de dessin* (Plate 1, No. 56), published ca. 1866–71

ABOVE: Kenyon Cox, *Sketch for Sculpture*, ca. 1896, graphite on paper, Library of Congress

Block in a figure drawing

Re-create the Degas drawing in the space opposite by finding the top, bottom, and halfway point of the figure. Look for key angles that describe your figure.

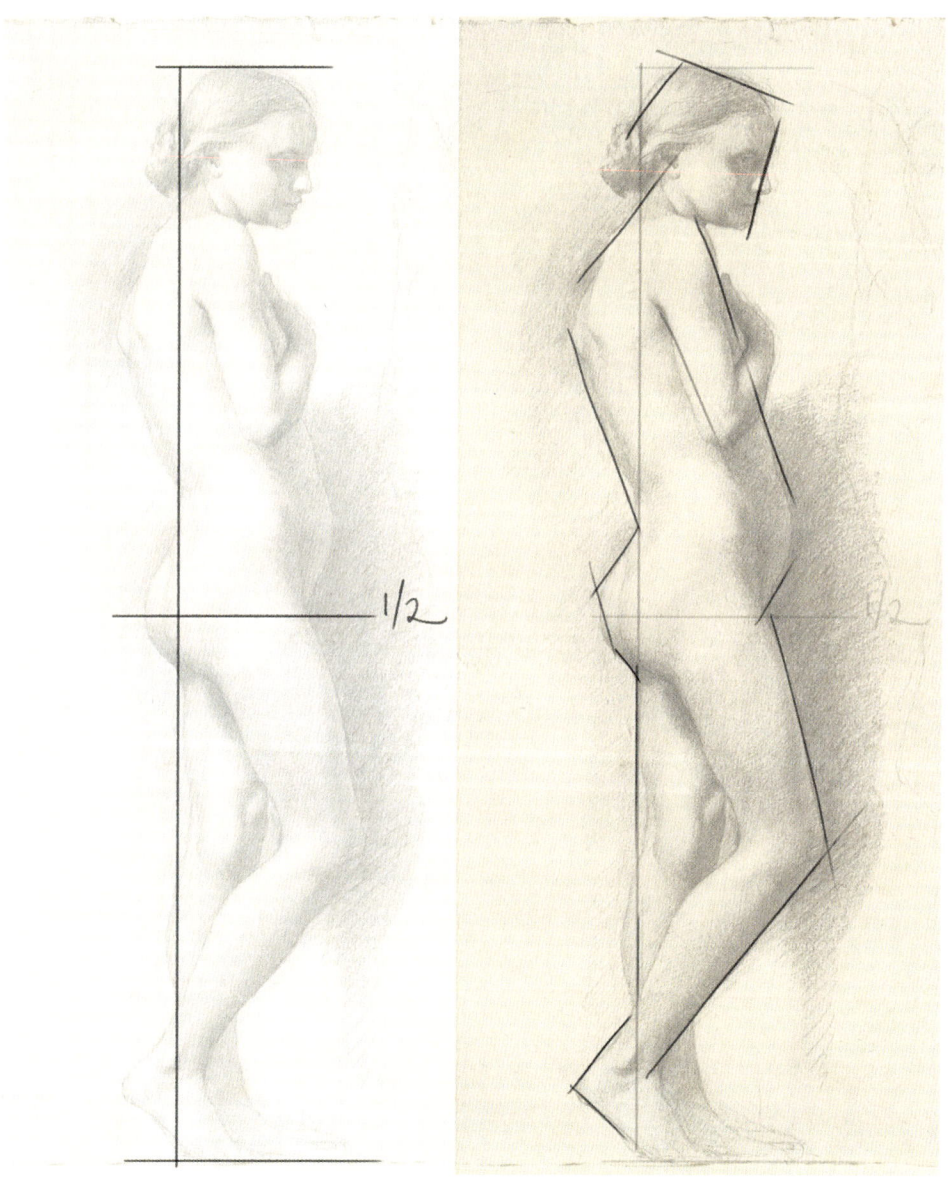

1/2

1/2

Edgar Degas, *Life Study of a Standing Nude*, ca. 1856–58, pencil on paper, 11 ½ x 8 ⅗ inches (29.1 x 21.8 cm), Sterling and Francine Clark Art Institute, Williamstown, Massachusetts. Image courtesy of the Art Renewal Center

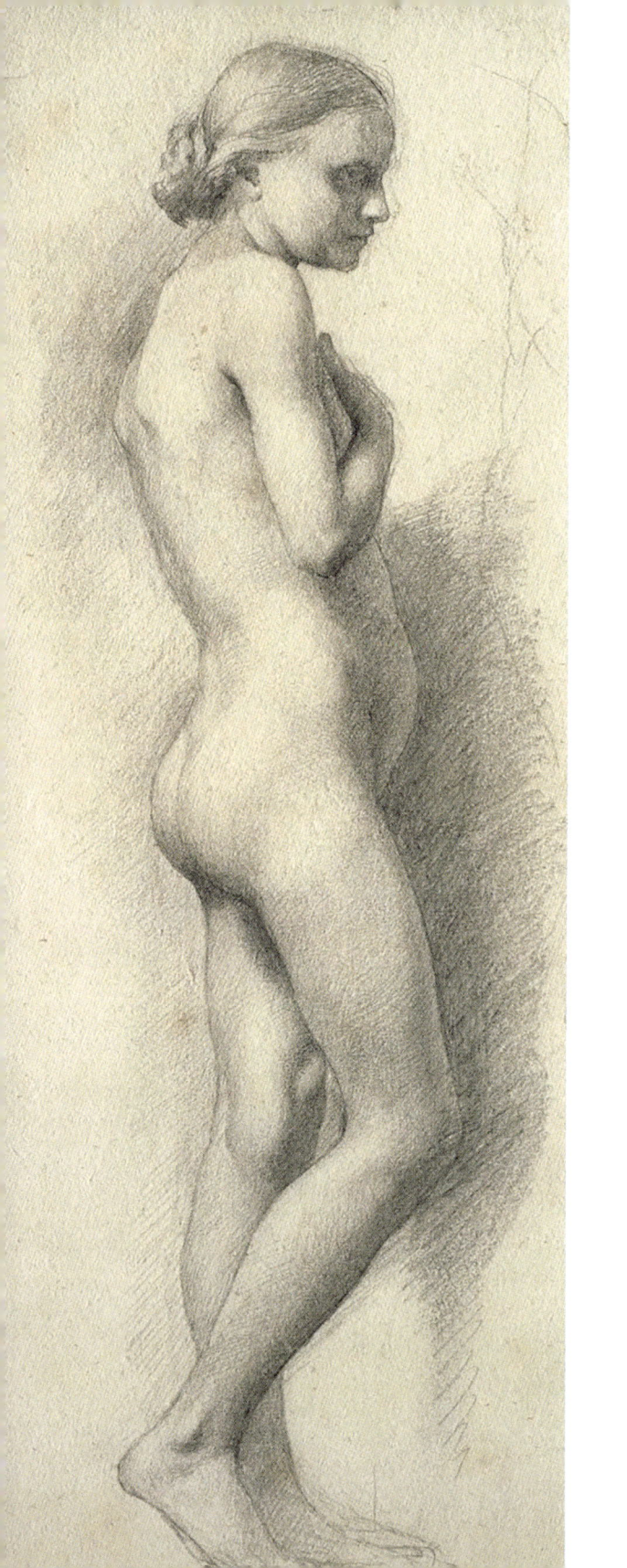

Tips and tilts

In this exercise, lightly re-create steps one and two seen below in the space opposite to find the tips and tilts of the figure.

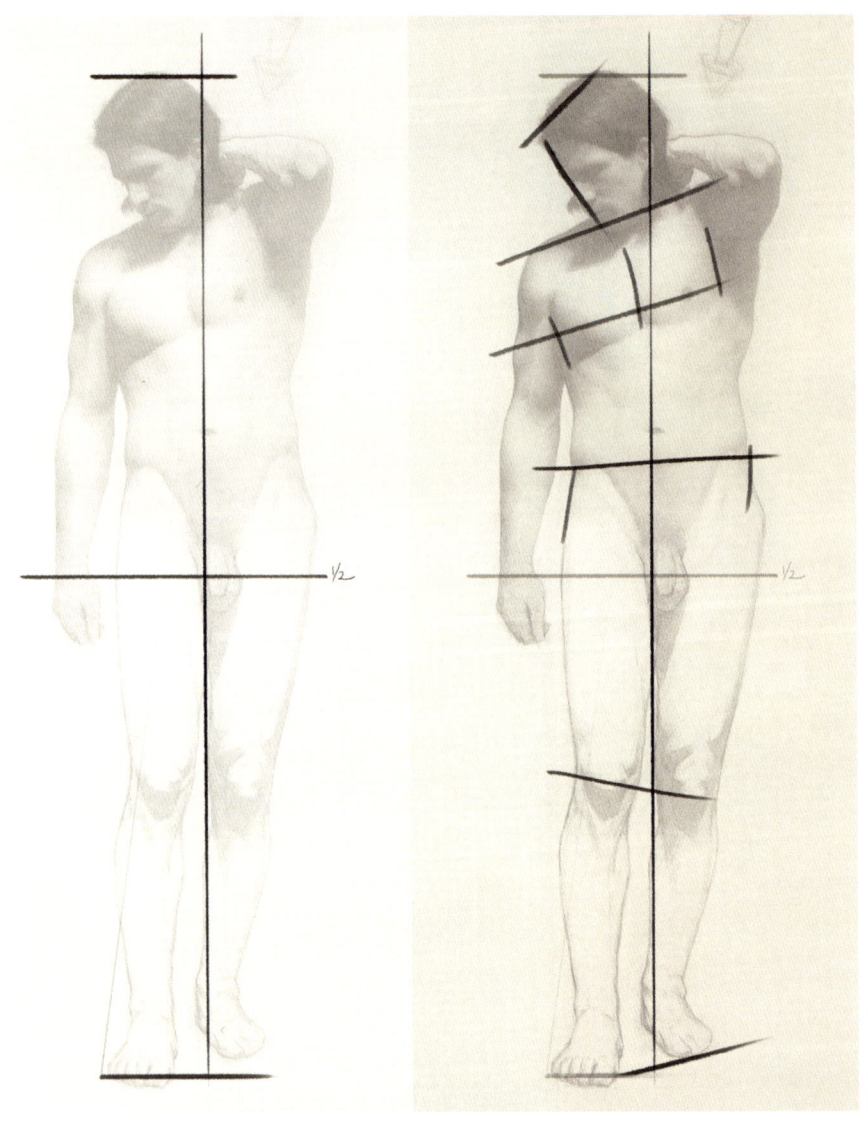

Samuel Hung, *Male Figure (Michael)*, 2011, graphite on paper, 23 ½ x 18 inches (59.7 x 45.7 cm)

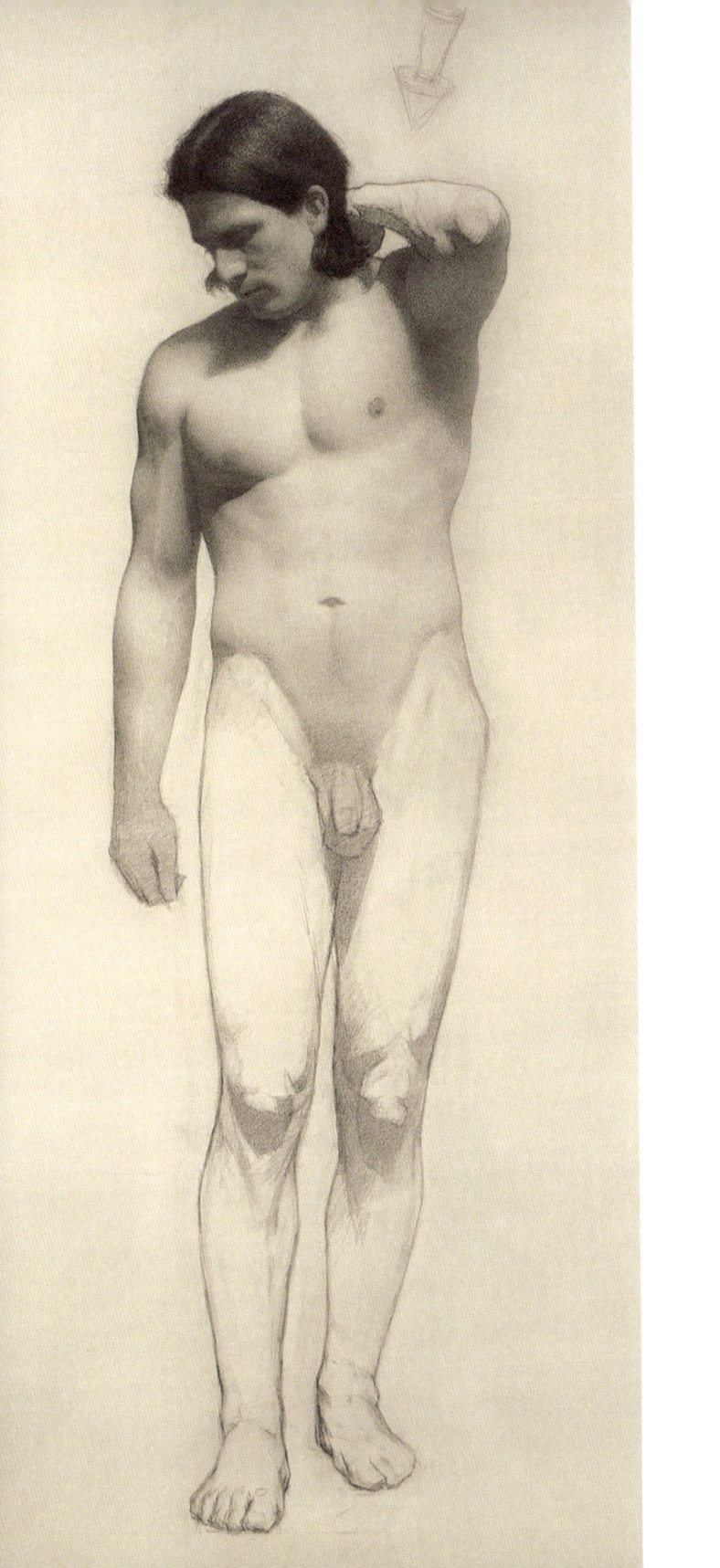

Measuring

In the Renaissance, figure drawing reached a high point of artistic achievement. Notable artists studied the human figure to uncover universal systems of proportion and copied idealized figures of Greco-Roman sculpture. Along the way, they established a canon of archetypal forms still referenced today.

Renaissance artists understood that having a standard reference of human proportion did not mean you were bound to create ideal figures. Rather, it provided a point of comparison to see how your subject conformed to (or differed from) convention. Even so, you would be surprised just how often our models conform to the same rules established hundreds of years ago. For example, in the drawing on the facing page, German Renaissance artist Albrecht Dürer maps out the proportions of a human hand. My left hand looks just like this, including what I thought was an idiosyncratic tilt of the tip of my middle finger to the left. When I draw someone's hand, this information will make me a keener observer.

Inspiration takes us only so far in the creation of a drawing. *Measuring* allows us to be more objective as we double-check our work. There is more than one way to measure, yet in essence, all measuring ensures that each part of our drawing is consistent with the whole and with our source.

To ease into the process of measuring, make your drawings the same size as the artwork you are copying so you can site your measurements directly. For example, to check widths, simply use your pencil to measure the width of the original and compare it with that of your drawing. If the original is four inches wide, yours should be as well. Checking distances and proportions using measurement allows you to objectively see if you are on the right path.

If your drawing is a different size from the one you are copying, you can measure another way. Take any unit of measure, such as a head, and use it to check your figure. If the drawing you are copying has two head lengths between the bottom of the chin and the navel but your drawing has three, something is off. Likewise, you can check width to height. For example, how does the width of the foot compare to the length of the head? Is it the same in both the original and your drawing?

To measure a real model (rather than a master copy), hold your pencil or a skewer with your arm outright, the skewer parallel to your body and perpendicular to the floor. Keep your elbow straight and shut the eye on the opposite side of the body from the skewer. Locate the top of your figure with the tip of the skewer and slide your thumb down until your nail rests upon the base of the chin. This will be your unit of measure: one head length. Keeping that unit locked in place, move your skewer down one head length. Where does it hit? (Often, near the nipples.) Once you get the hang of it, try using that same unit of measure to see how many times the length of the head goes into the width of the shoulders.

To check vertical and horizontal alignments, making sure everything is lining up as it should (such as the head over the feet), you can use a plumb line. This is a thread with a small weight at the bottom.

Once, while listening to an interview, I heard a master violin maker say to his apprentice, "Go slowly. We are in a hurry." He meant, of course, that the quickest way to get something done well and without mistakes is to proceed carefully. This stage of measuring your drawing is slow, requiring checking and double-checking. Take your time, even if it means you can't finish your drawing in one sitting. By checking your horizontals, verticals, and a few angles to make sure all the parts align, you will be able to weed out most of your mistakes. Over time, your eye will improve and this stage will become quicker and more intuitive.

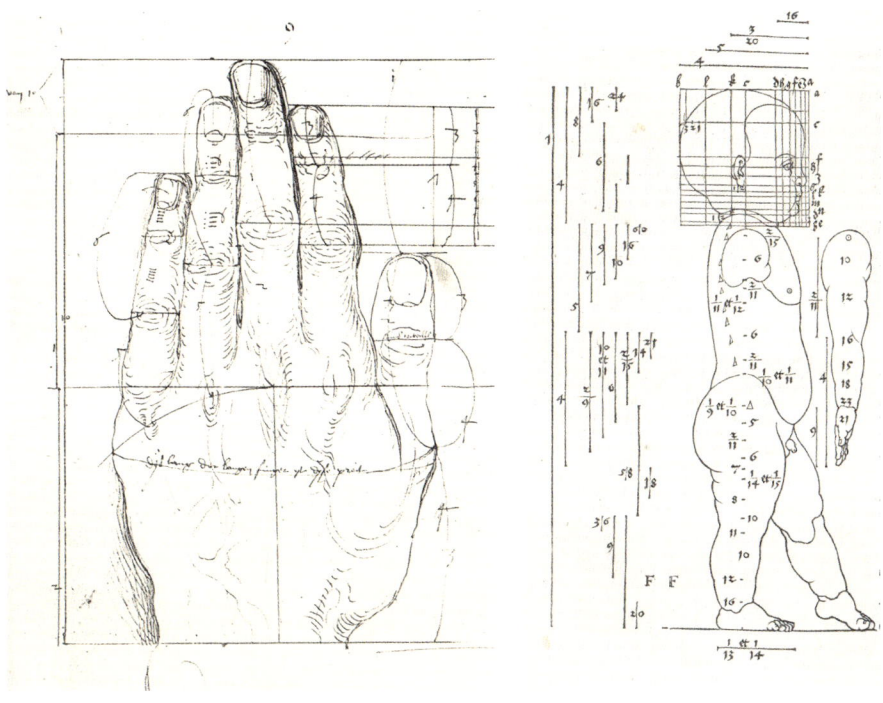

LEFT: Albrecht Dürer, *Dürer's Left Hand*, 11 ½ x 8 ⅛ inches (29.4 x 20.8 cm), published in *The Dresden Sketchbook*. Image courtesy of the Art Renewal Center

RIGHT: Albrecht Dürer, *Baby in Proportion*, from *Four Books on Human Proportion*. Image courtesy of the Art Renewal Center

Find the measurements

Study the drawing by Leonardo da Vinci shown below then re-create its measurement on the contour of the head provided opposite. Start by finding the box around the head (from the nose to the back of the head, and from the top of the head to the chin). See how Leonardo subdivided the head into thirds: from the chin to under the nose, from under the nose to the brow, and from the brow to the top of the head. Continue to find the rest of the measurements.

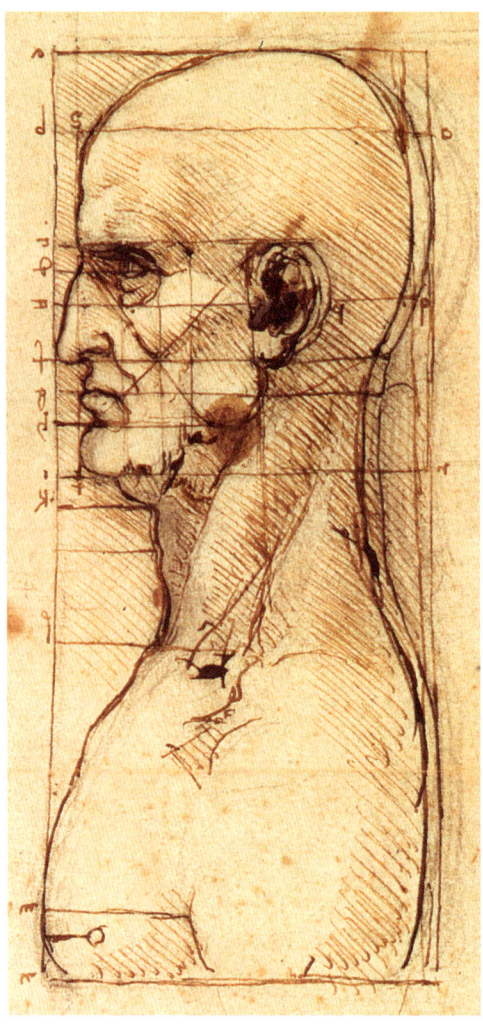

Leonardo da Vinci, *Head of a Man with Scheme of Its Proportions* (detail), ca. 1490, pen and ink, 11 x 9 inches (27.9 x 23.3 cm), Accademia, Venice, Italy. Image courtesy of Scala/Art Resource, New York

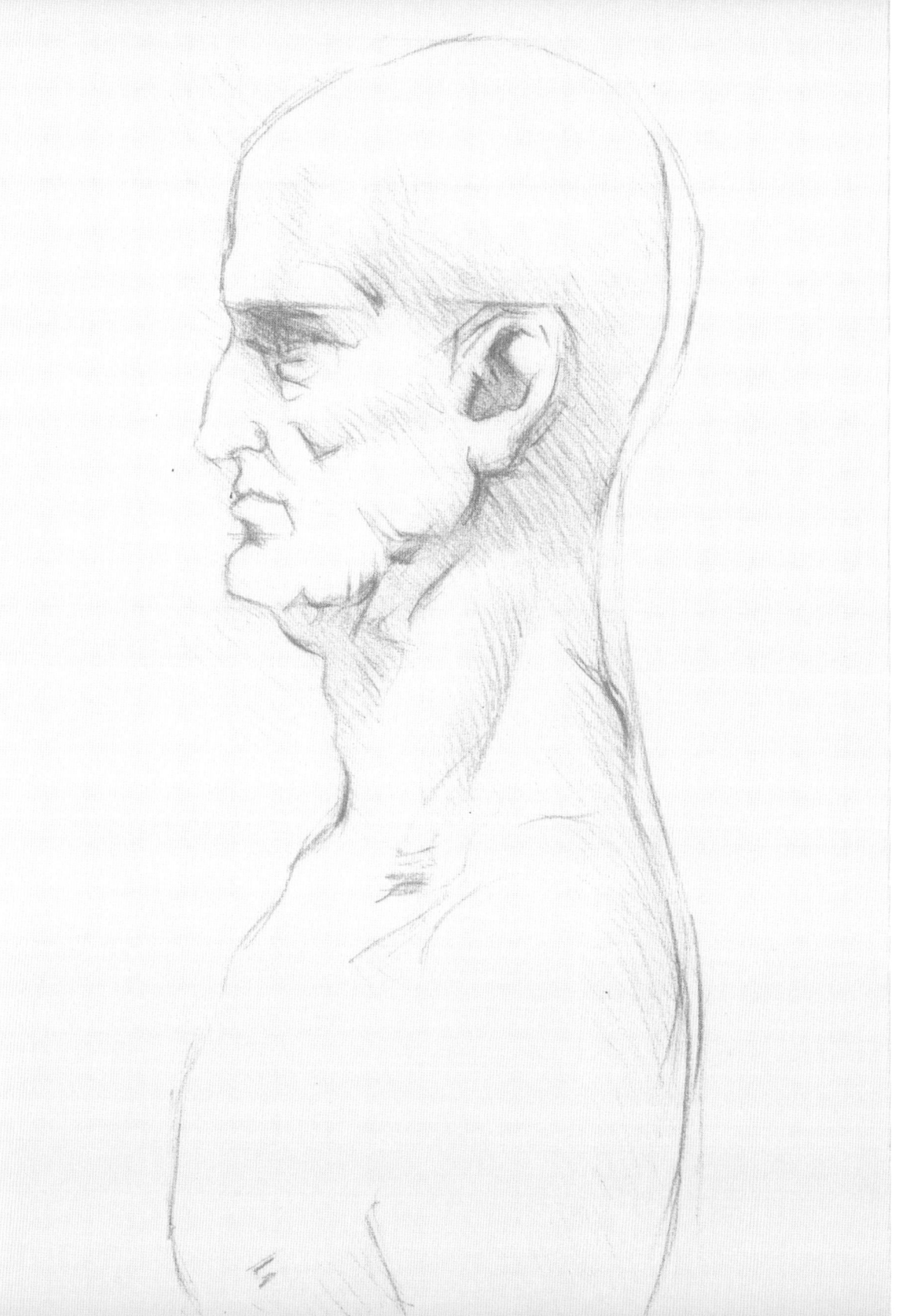

Practice measuring

On the ghosted image below, mark ticks at each head length to see how many heads high the figure is. Next, copy the drawing opposite and on page 50 by finding the top, bottom, and halfway point before freely sketching and then checking your measurements.

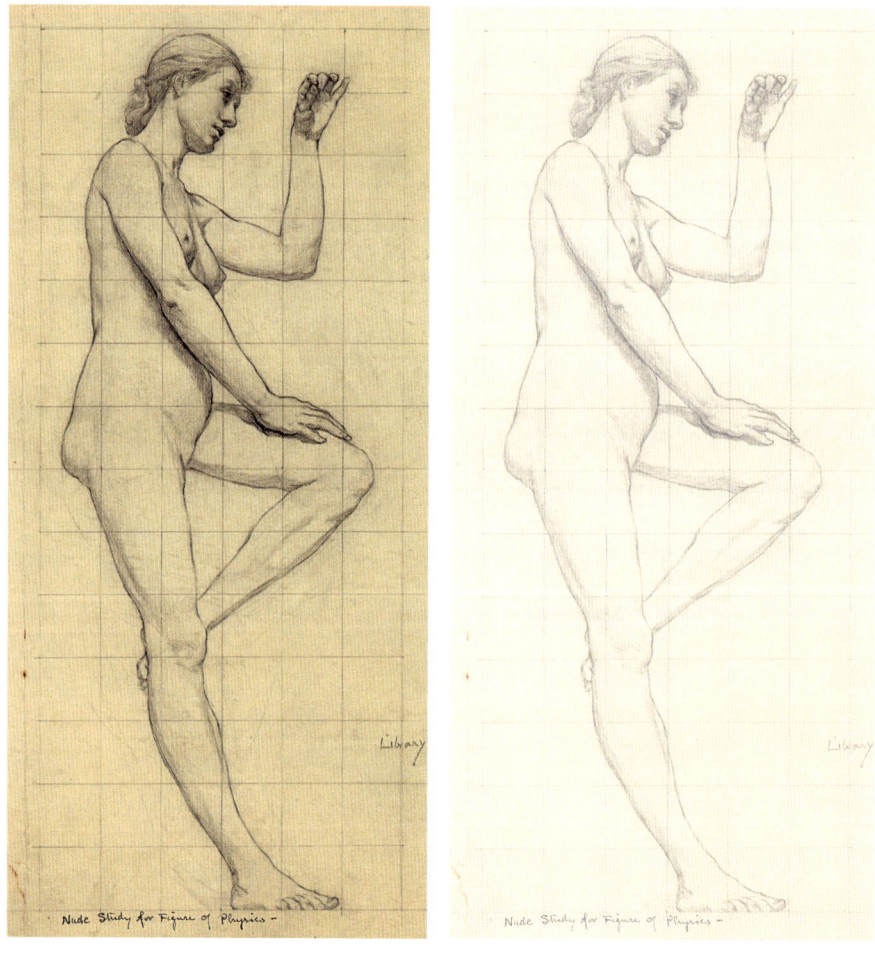

ABOVE: Kenyon Cox, *Nude Study of Physics*, ca. 1896, graphite on paper, size unknown, Library of Congress

OPPOSITE: Kenyon Cox, *Nude Study for Figure of Botany*, ca. 1896, size unknown, Library of Congress

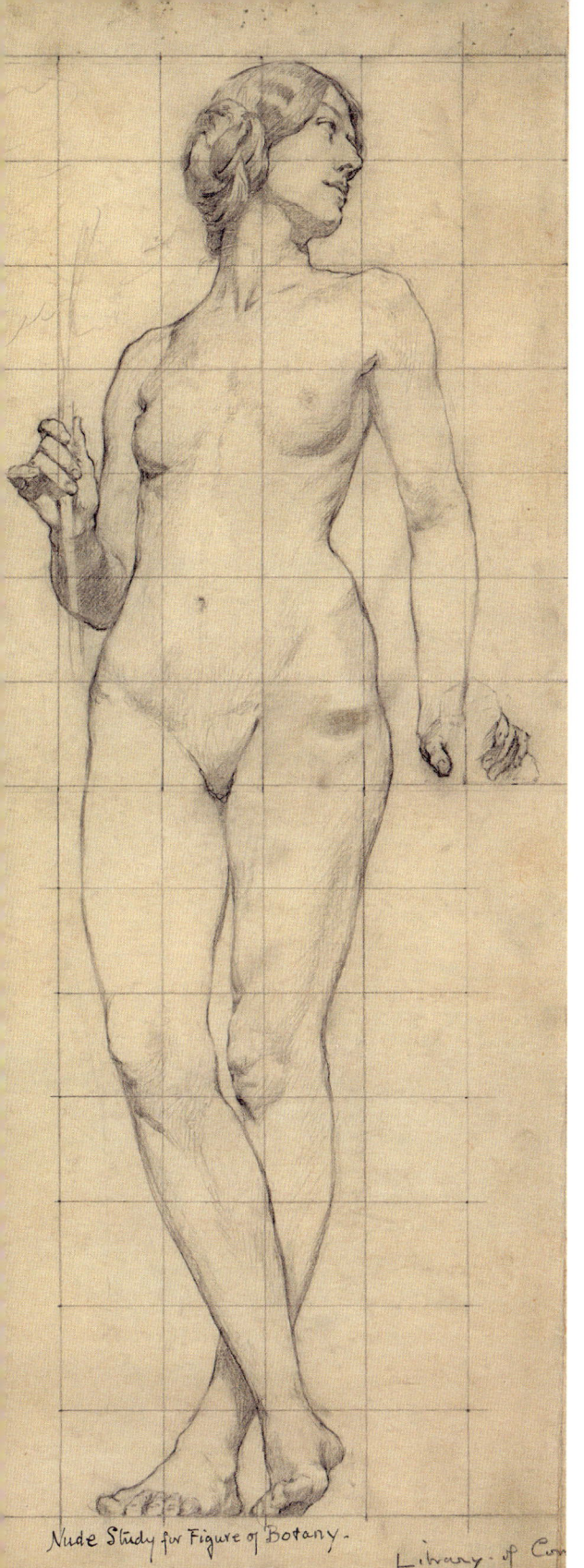

Nude Study for Figure of Botany.

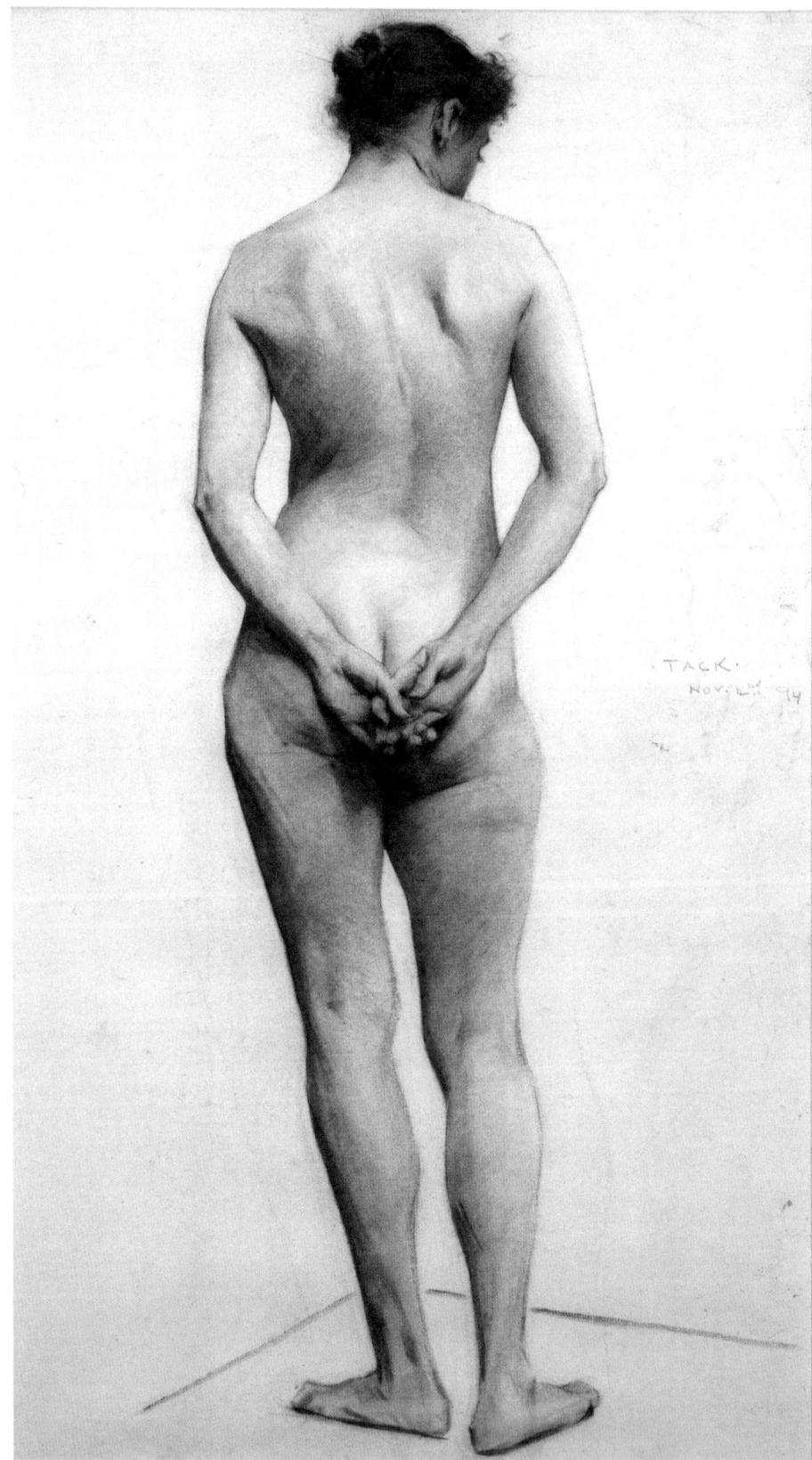

Augustus Vincent Tack,
Untitled, 1984, charcoal on
paper, 24 x 15 inches
(61 x 38.1 cm). Image courtesy
of the Art Students League of
New York

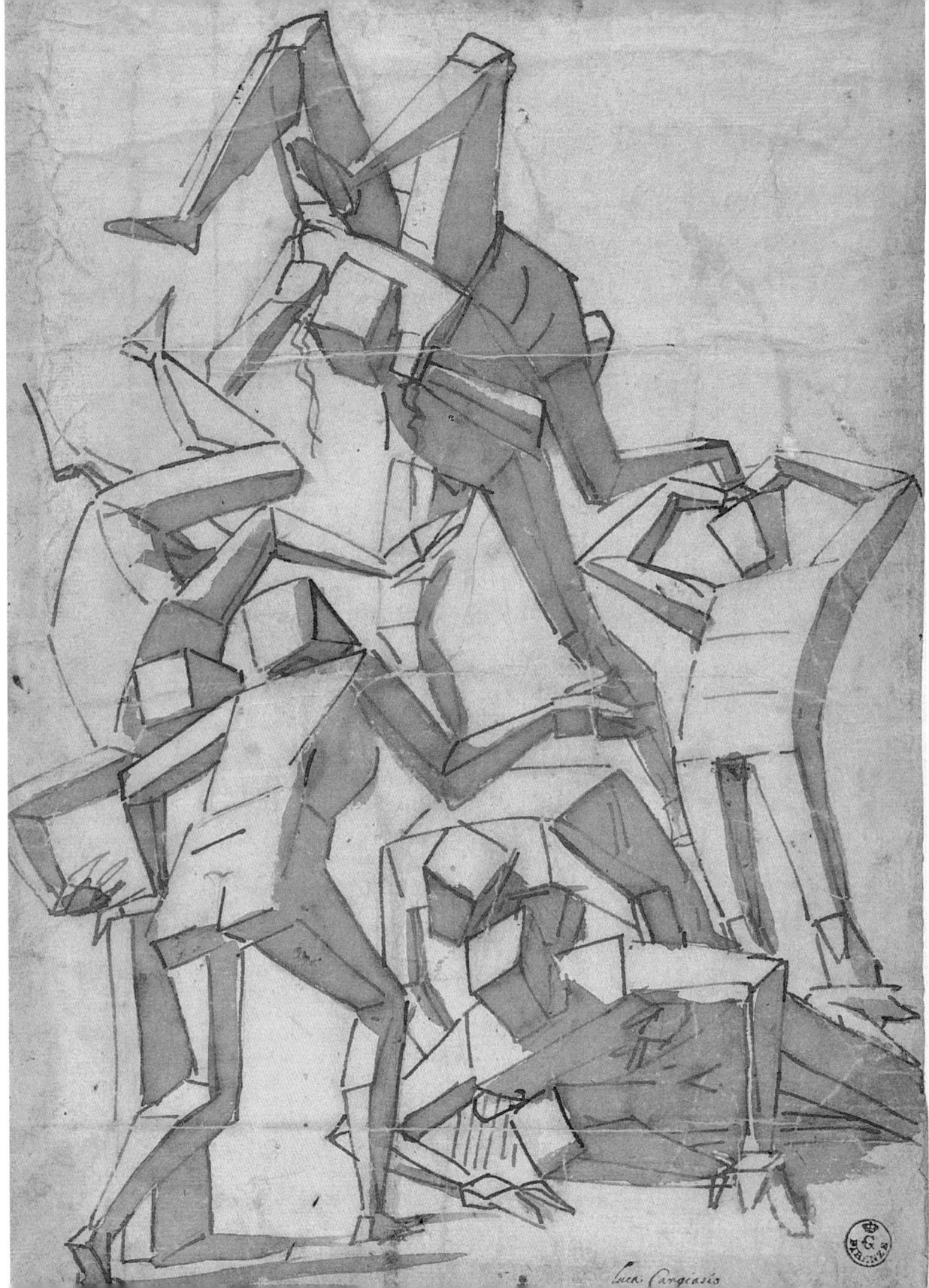

Luca Cangiasio

THREE

VOLUME

In the case of the human figure it is impossible properly to understand its action and draw it in a way that shall give a powerful impression without a knowledge of the mechanics of its construction.

—HAROLD SPEED, *THE PRACTICE AND SCIENCE OF DRAWING*

For my eighth birthday party, my mom organized a game: she walked my friends and me through an obstacle course, and then blindfolded us and instructed us to navigate it one by one. Each person who completed the course removed her blindfold to watch the next person. It was hilarious watching kids contort themselves to go around the chair, or crawl under the table. Of course, the trick was that nothing was there. All of the obstacles had been removed and we made space for things that did not exist except in memory.

Drawing figures with volume is similar to navigating that childhood obstacle course: as the children made room for the chair, we need to make room for our figures. We want to *feel* the back of the figure even if we see only the front. Our heads must have weight no matter what the vantage point. We want our two-dimensional drawings to have the appearance of real mass and volume. For that, we must have an innate sense of the head's weight and how much space it requires, the girth of the ribcage, and the mass of the pelvis. We can envision, with our eyes closed, the space our figures inhabit. To start seeing volume, practice drawing simple geometric shapes, such as cubes, cylinders, and spheres.

The human figure is challenging to draw because it can appear somewhat soft and formless; parts of the body overlap and look like oranges stuffed into a stocking. It is hard to draw the figure without a mental construct of what it "should" look like, and in the absence of a template we can end up chasing the contour.

OPPOSITE: Luca Cambiaso, *Study of Cubic Figures*, ca.1560–65, pen and brown ink, Gabinetto dei Disegni e delle Stampe, Uffizi, Florence, Italy. Image courtesy of the Art Renewal Center

The key to creating volume in a drawing is to clearly express the height, width, and depth of the figure. One useful way to envision this is to treat the head, ribcage, and pelvis as simple blocks that can be tipped and tilted in space. If well seen and placed, these three major masses of the body give us a believable sense of three-dimensional space.

The drawings in this chapter lead you through different ways to block in the head, ribcage, and pelvis to help your figure feel volumetric. Basically, you are answering questions such as: "Am I looking up or down at my subject? Is he turning away from me?" Note that we don't start our life drawings from blocks. They are purely practice forms to help us see the planes of the body. In our final work we lose the boxes but keep the feeling of space they inhabit.

Finding the masses of the body

Let's look at each of the three masses in turn. The bony landmarks of the body described on page 38 can help us find these boxy components. Remember, this is art, not science, and these descriptions are used for general understanding rather than as fixed rules.

First, the head. The top of the head is simply the crown. The side planes begin just as you feel the eyes, around to the temporal region of the skull, and extending to the back. (Put your hands flat alongside your head, covering your ears, and feel the flatness of this plane.) The underside of the head runs under the jaw. The front of the face is found from just above the hairline to the bottom of the chin. To see which way the box of the face is tipping, look at the centerline of the face, which starts between the eyes and runs down the nose to the center of the chin. This straight line is crossed by the perpendicular line of the eyes. For examples of the centerline, see Kevin Chen's drawings on page 74 and Charles Barque's image on page 70.

To find the mass of the ribcage, find the "T" formed by the horizontal line of the clavicle and perpendicular sternum. The clavicle can be represented by a straight line that becomes the top edge of your box. (See Luca Cambiaso's *Study of Cubic Figures* on page 52 to visualize the body simplified into planed forms.) Next, determine if you can see the top of the shoulders (think of the plane of the shoulders seen from above as the top of your box), which we imagine as a flat plane. Instead of the roundness you feel as you run your hand from the top of your shoulder to the side of your arm, imagine a square edge. Likewise, the back can be conceived of as a flat plane. These formalizations help us avoid being distracted by small forms until we understand the larger ones.

To find the side plane of the ribcage, lift your arm up and feel with your other hand the stretch of skin that runs from your armpit to the top of your waist; this can be simplified as one plane. The back of the ribcage is divided down the center by the spinal column and can be formalized as a single plane up to the shoulder. If the arms are relaxed and hanging down, you can draw a straight line from shoulder to shoulder across the back. However, arms have such a wide range of movement, it's rare to have a perfect alignment between the shoulder line and sides of the body from the back. A figure at rest standing straight will have the shoulders thrusting back and the bottom of the ribcage tipping forward, as in Geoffrey Flack's demonstration on pages 60 and 62.

For the pelvis, find the front by putting your index fingers on your hipbones and imagining a straight line stretching from one finger to the other. Shift your weight from one leg to the other and see how that line tips. This helps you see how your hips tip to the left or right. The front plane of the pelvis runs from your hipbone to about one hand span down to the bottom of your groin area. To find the side of the pelvic box, place your thumbs on your hipbones and your palms resting on the sides of your hips. The underside of the pelvis can be seen only from the side or back and corresponds to the shelf under your bottom. The standing pelvis at rest will be tipped forward. If you stand with good posture, you can feel your ribcage and shoulders thrusting back, your tummy straight, and your pelvis tipping forward, mirroring the curve of your spine.

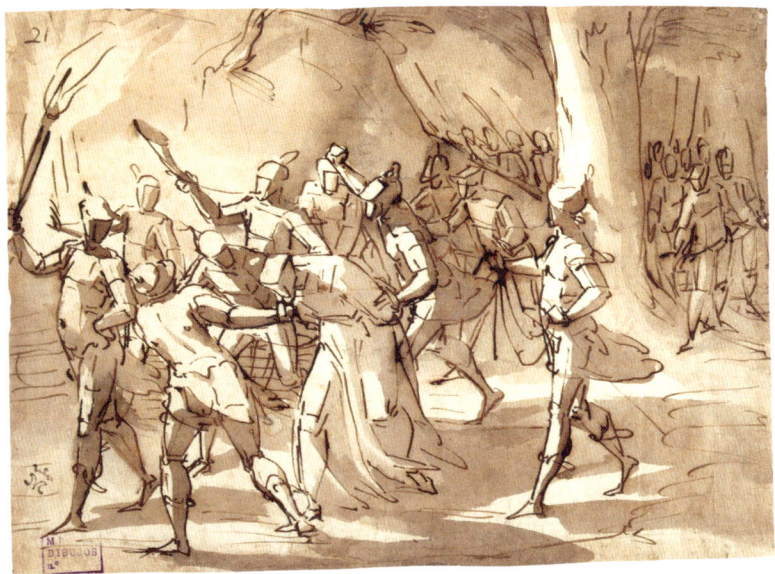

Luca Cambiaso, *Prendimiento de Cristo*, 1585, gouache and feather, prepared in pencil, Agrisada ink, and brown ink on yellowish paper, 8 ⅓ x 12 inches (21.2 x 30 cm), Museo Nacional del Prado, Madrid. Image courtesy of The Art Renewal Center

Cubed forms

Draw these boxy and egg-shaped versions of the ribcage and pelvis for figures in various positions. Notice how in a normal standing posture, the ribcage and pelvis tip away from one another. For more practice drawing boxes, try sketching a matchbox from different angles.

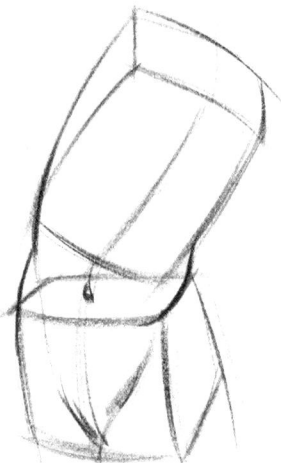 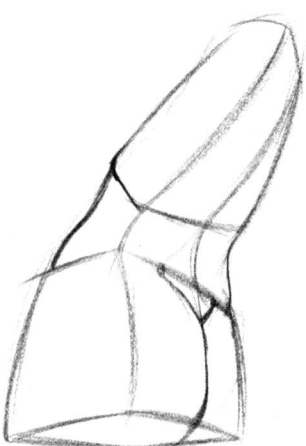 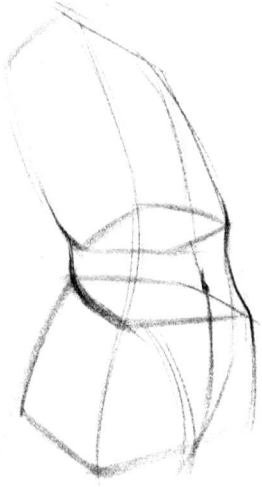

Stanislav Prokopenko, *Robobean sketch*. Image courtesy of proko.com

Notice the progression from box to a more defined ribcage as "bucket shaped" for the pelvis to the rounded anatomical forms of the body.

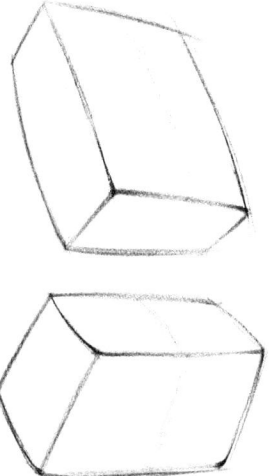
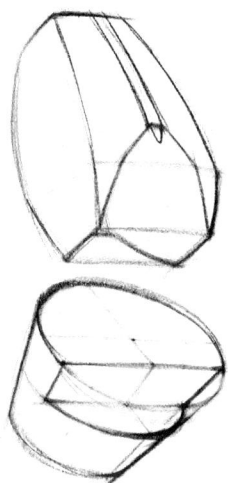
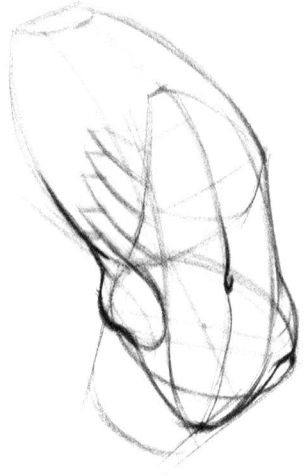

The cubed figure

Re-create the figures here and on the following pages in the spaces provided. Start by marking the placement of the head and feet to find the height for each figure, then find the action

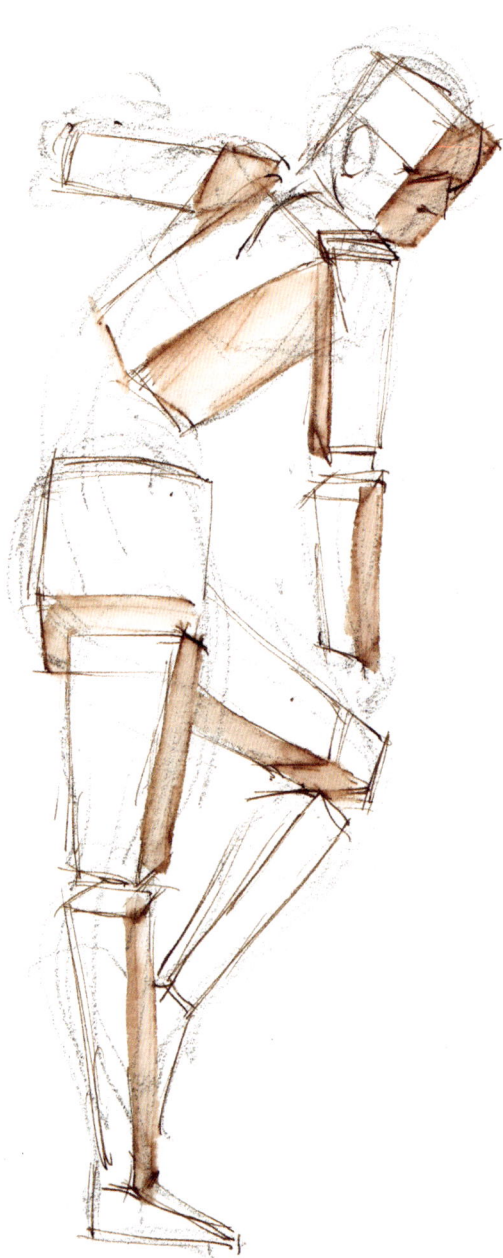

line. For the figures opposite and below, identify the planes that show the top, bottom, and sides. Look at the artist's initial gesture drawing seen lightly under the cubes.

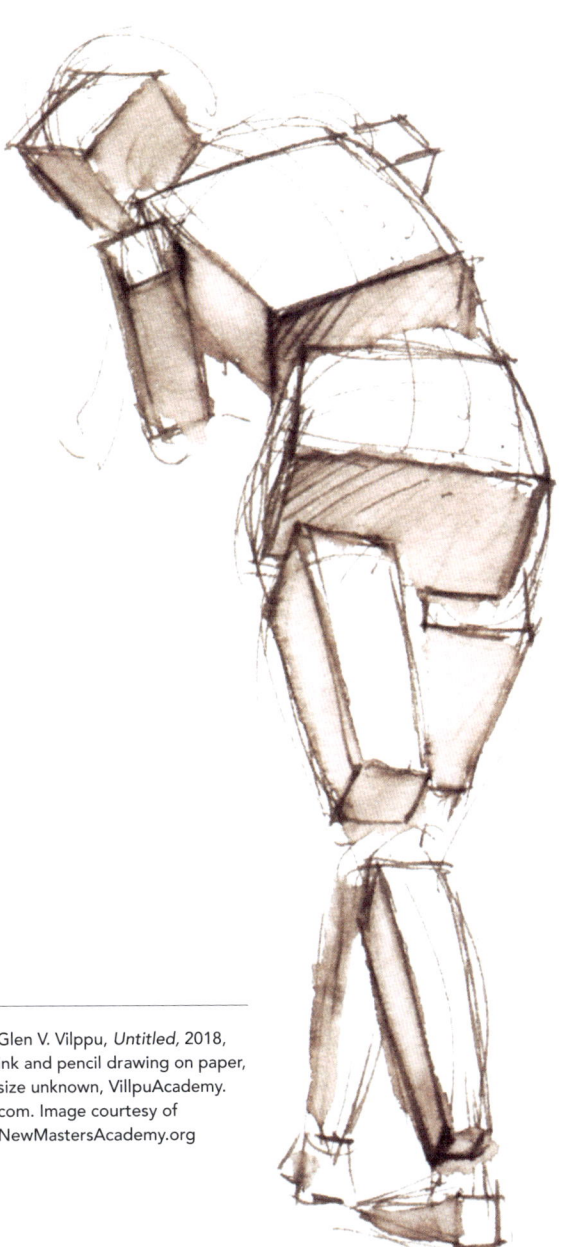

Glen V. Vilppu, *Untitled*, 2018, ink and pencil drawing on paper, size unknown, VillpuAcademy.com. Image courtesy of NewMastersAcademy.org

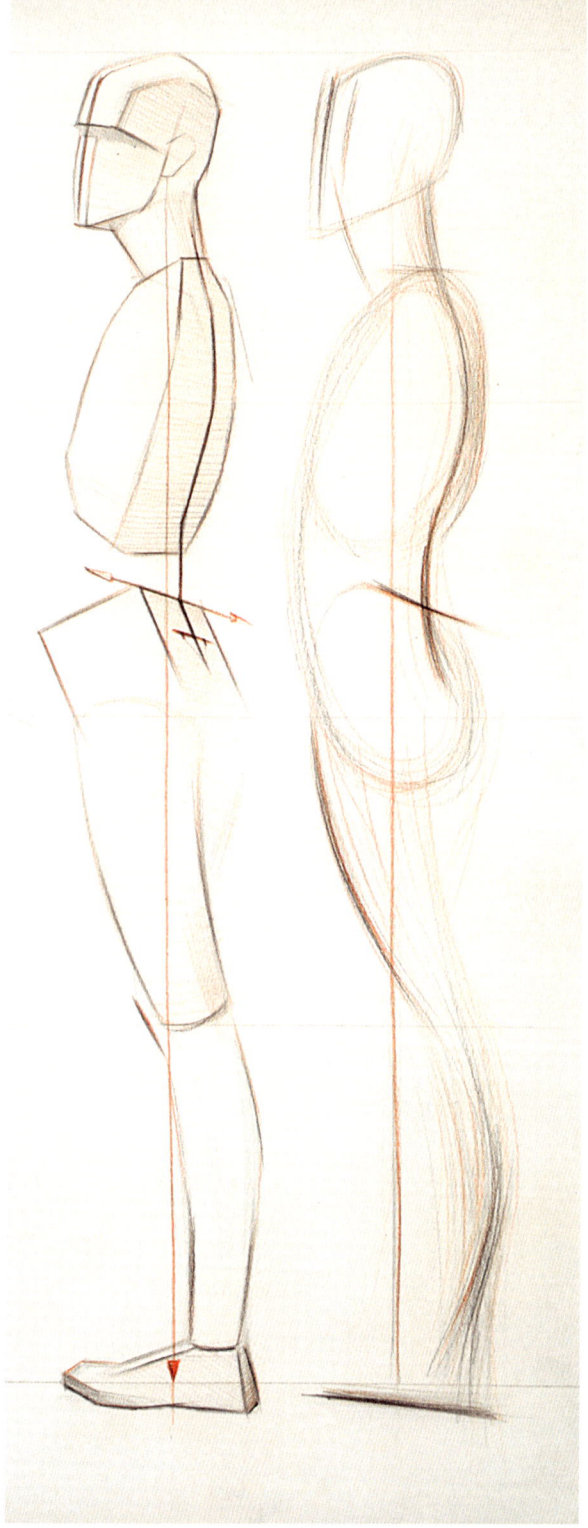

Geoffrey Flack, *Untitled structural drawing demonstration*, 2015, graphite and colored pencil, 24 x 19 inches (61 x 48.3 cm)

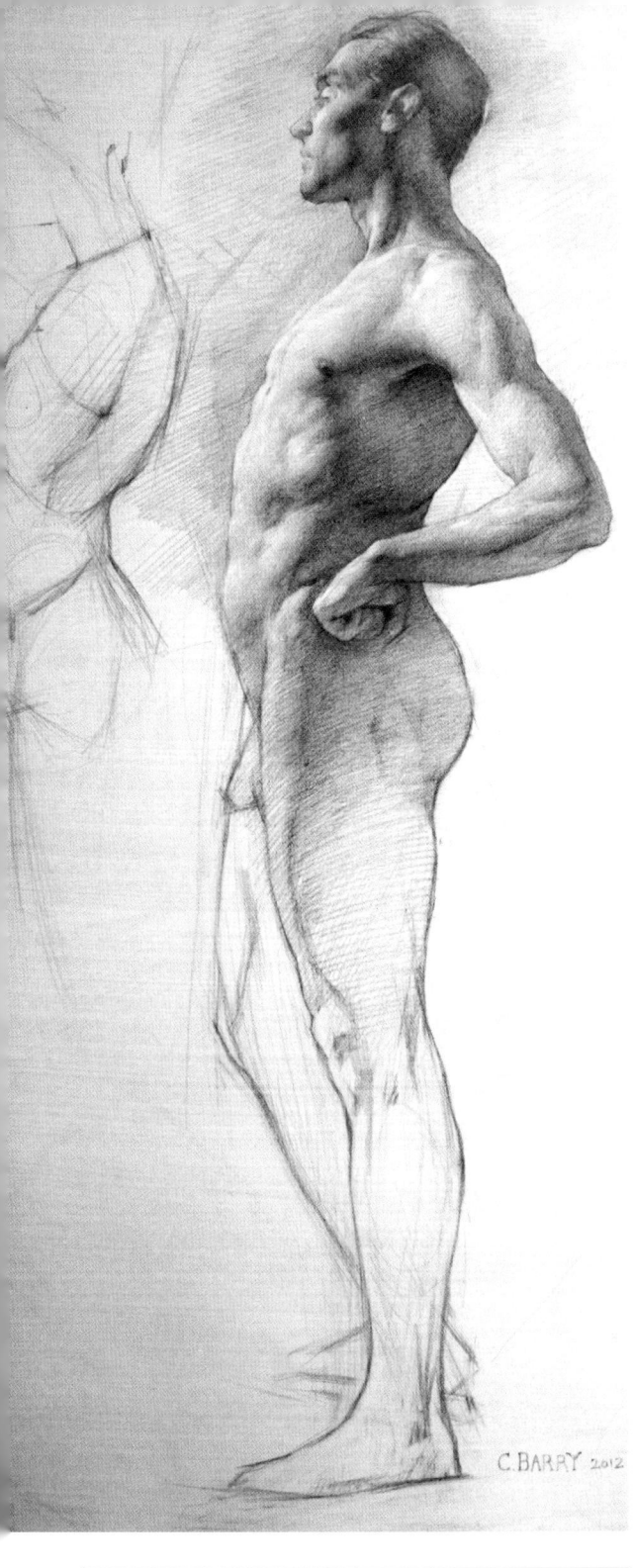

Colleen Barry, *Standing Male Nude,* 2013, graphite on toned paper, 2
4 x 18 inches (61 x 45.6 cm)

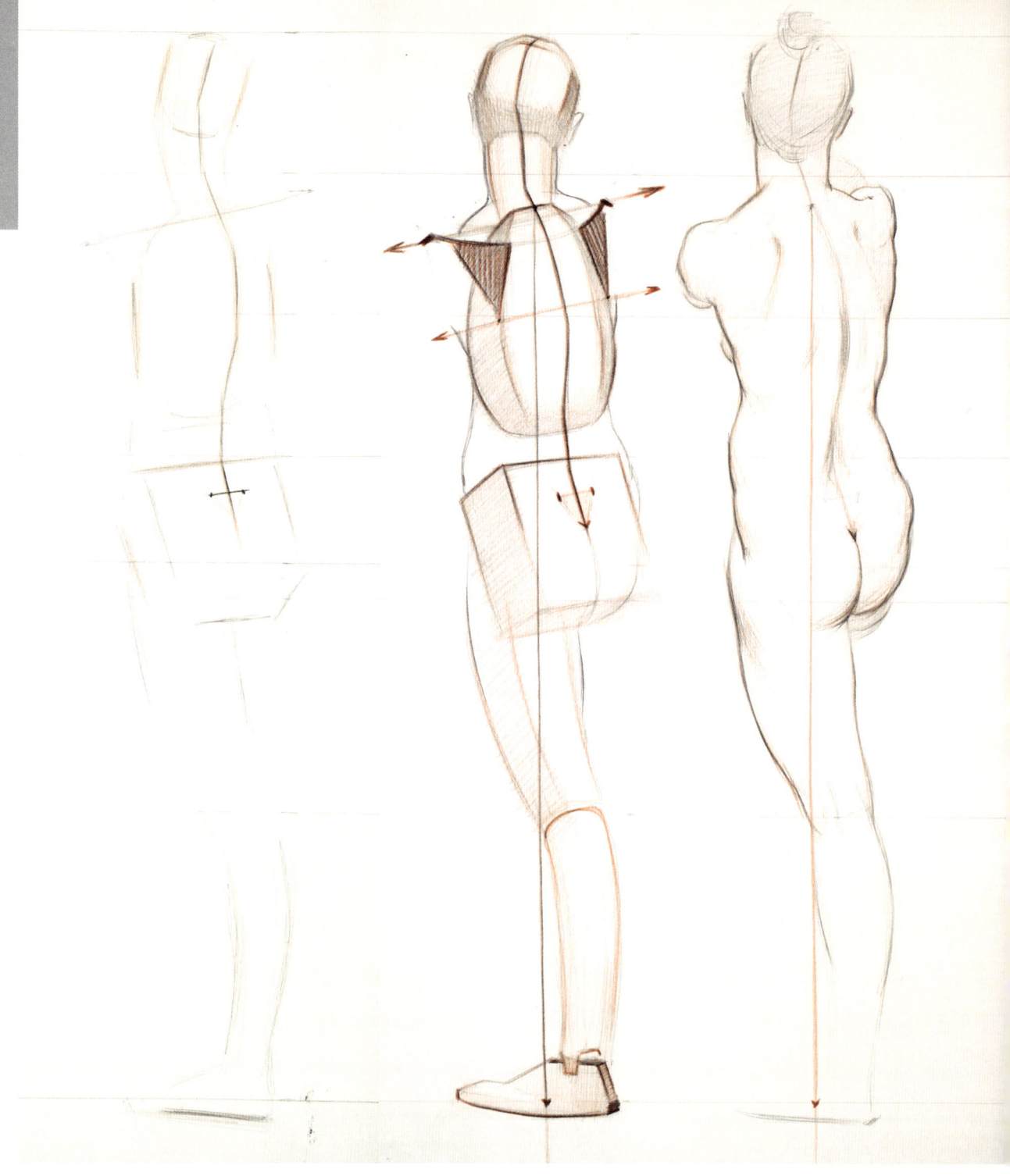

Geoffrey Flack, *Untitled structural drawing demonstration,* 2015, graphite and colored pencil, 19 x 24 inches
(48.3 x 61 cm)

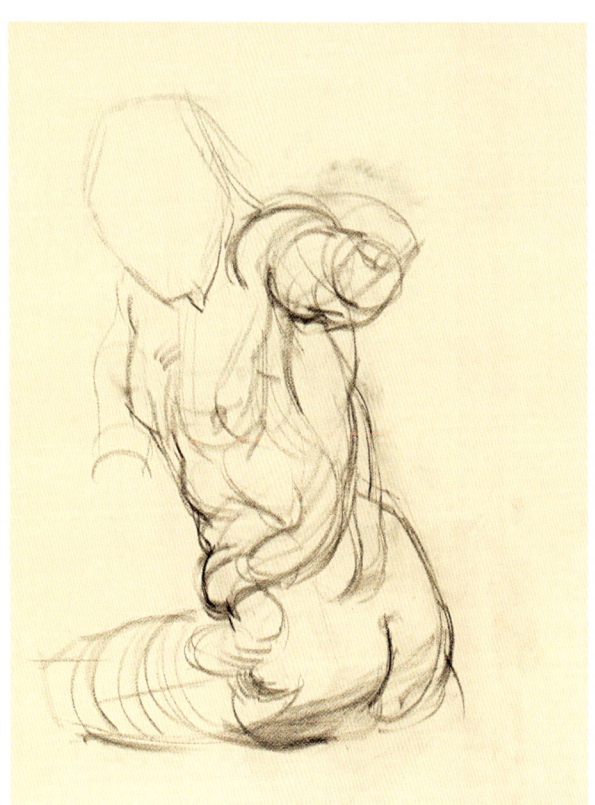
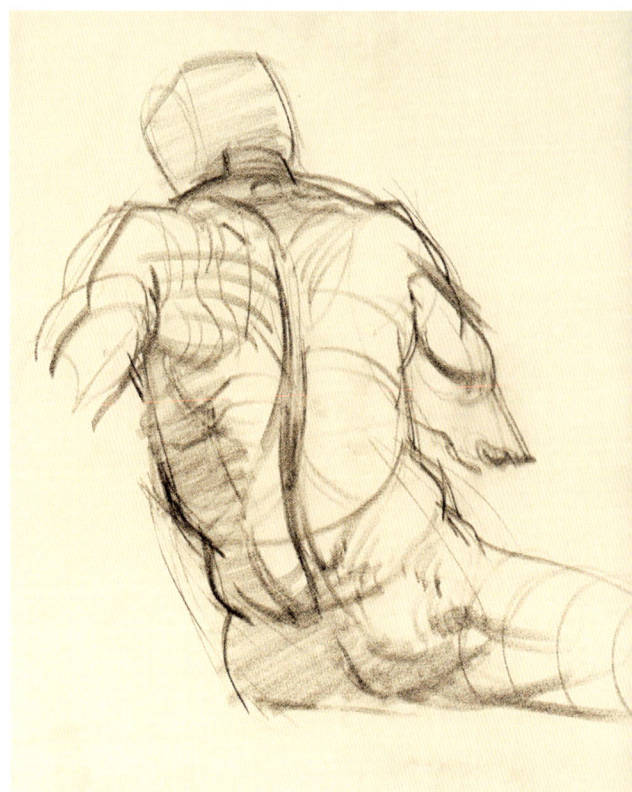

Joshua Jacobo, *Untitled*, 2017, Conté pencil on paper. Image courtesy of NewMastersAcademy.org

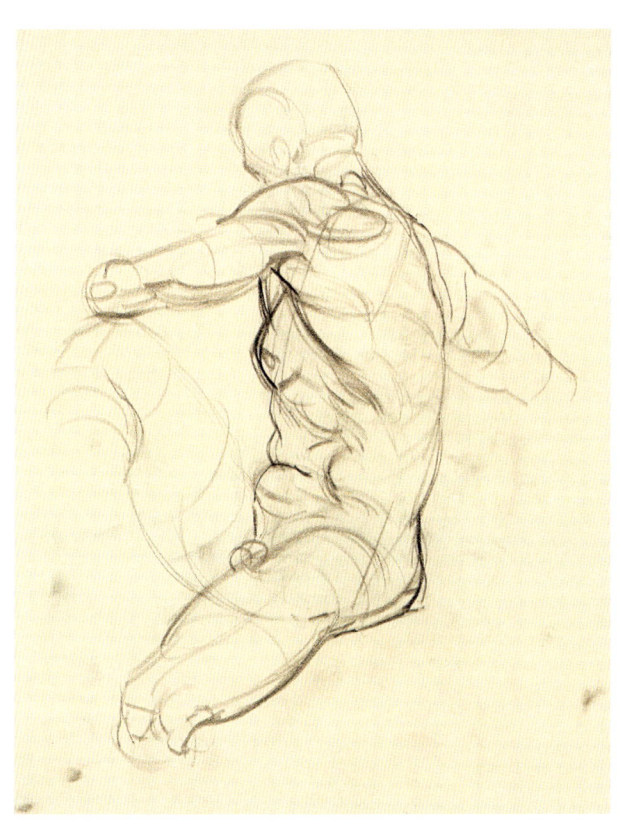
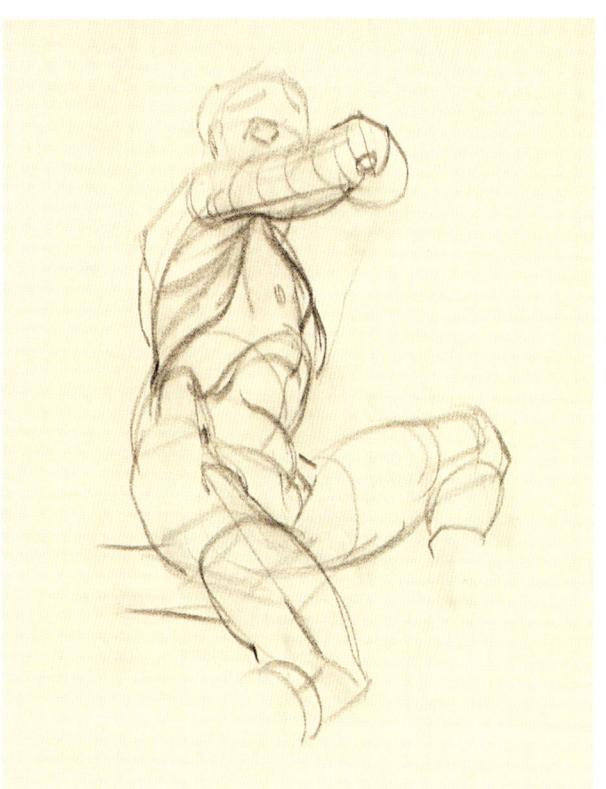

Find the cubed forms in the figures

Follow the examples to find the boxes that locate the heads, ribcages, and pelvises of the figures in Rubens's *Sketch for Fall of the Damned* and draw them on the ghosted version. Don't worry about getting the right answer; just take your best guess.

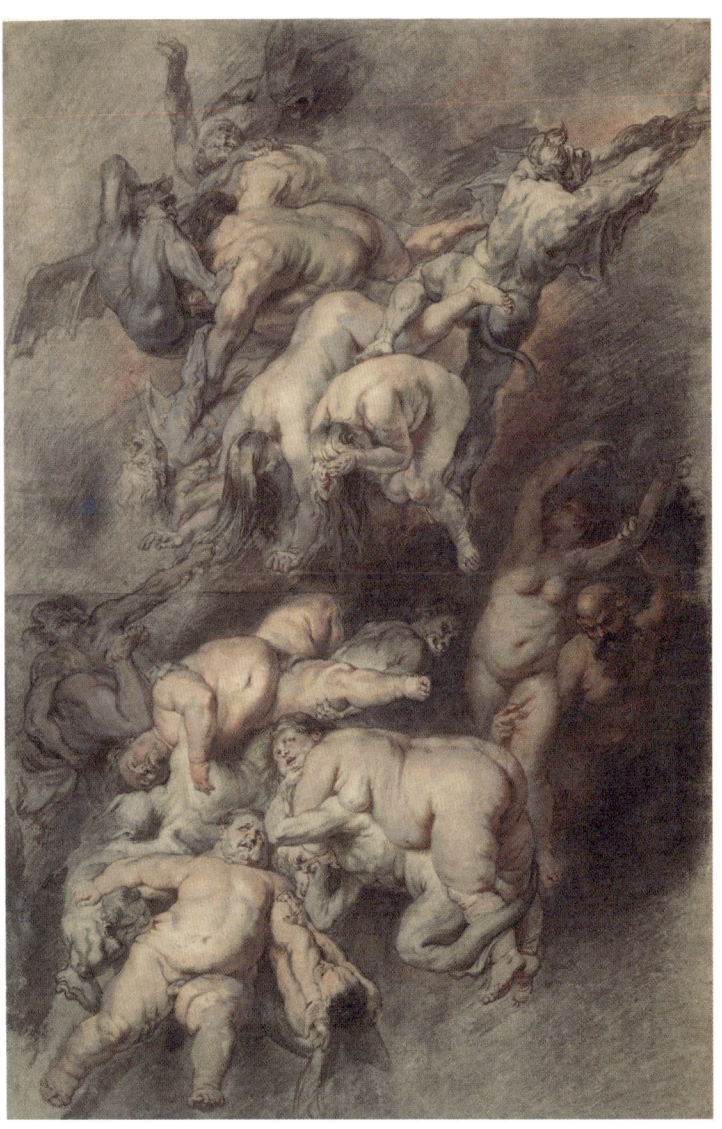

Peter Paul Rubens, *Sketch for Fall of the Damned*, ca. 1614–18, black and red chalk with gray wash, 27 ⁹/₁₀ x 18 ⁷/₁₀ inches (70.9 x 47.4 cm), British Museum, London

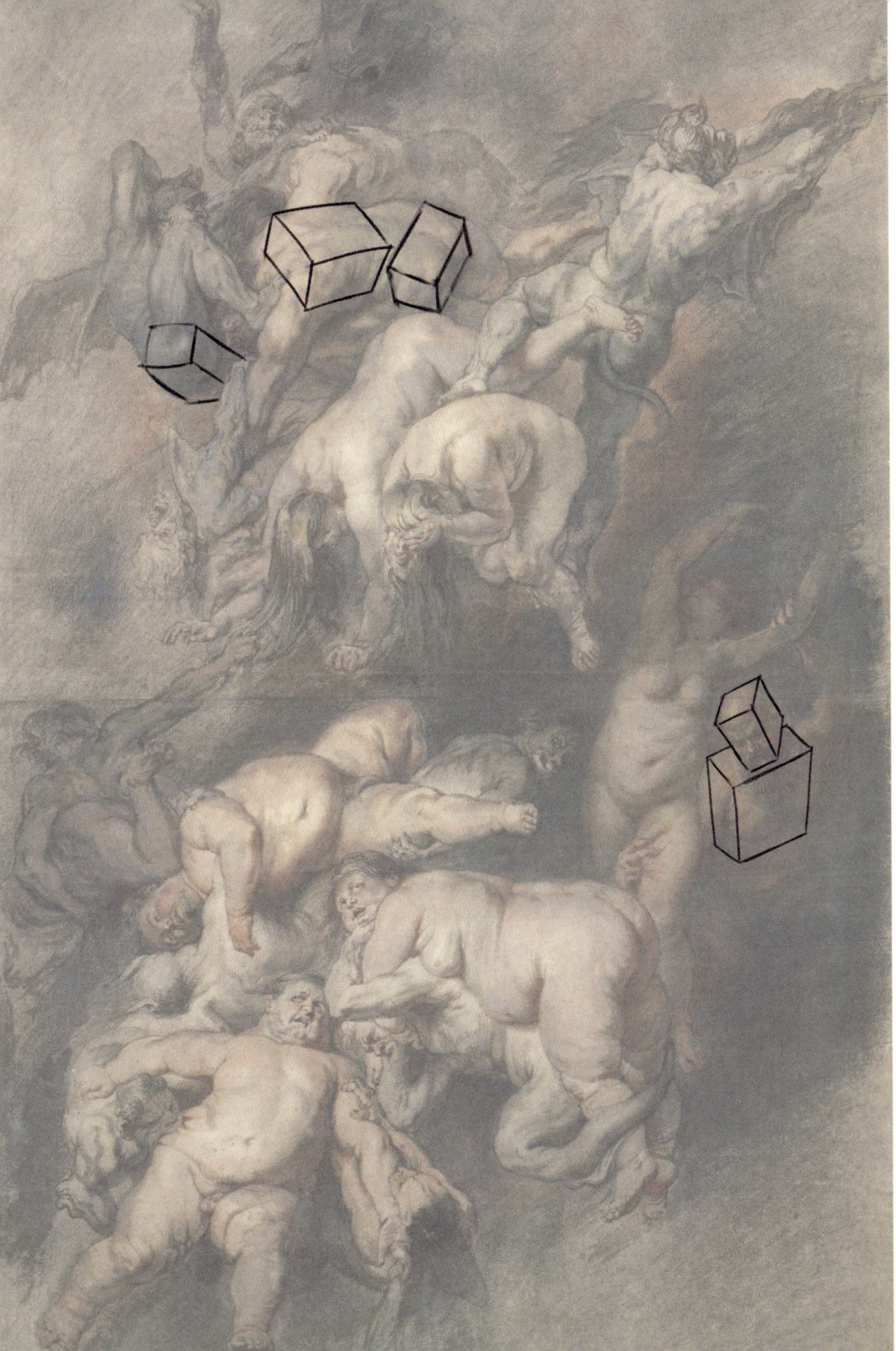

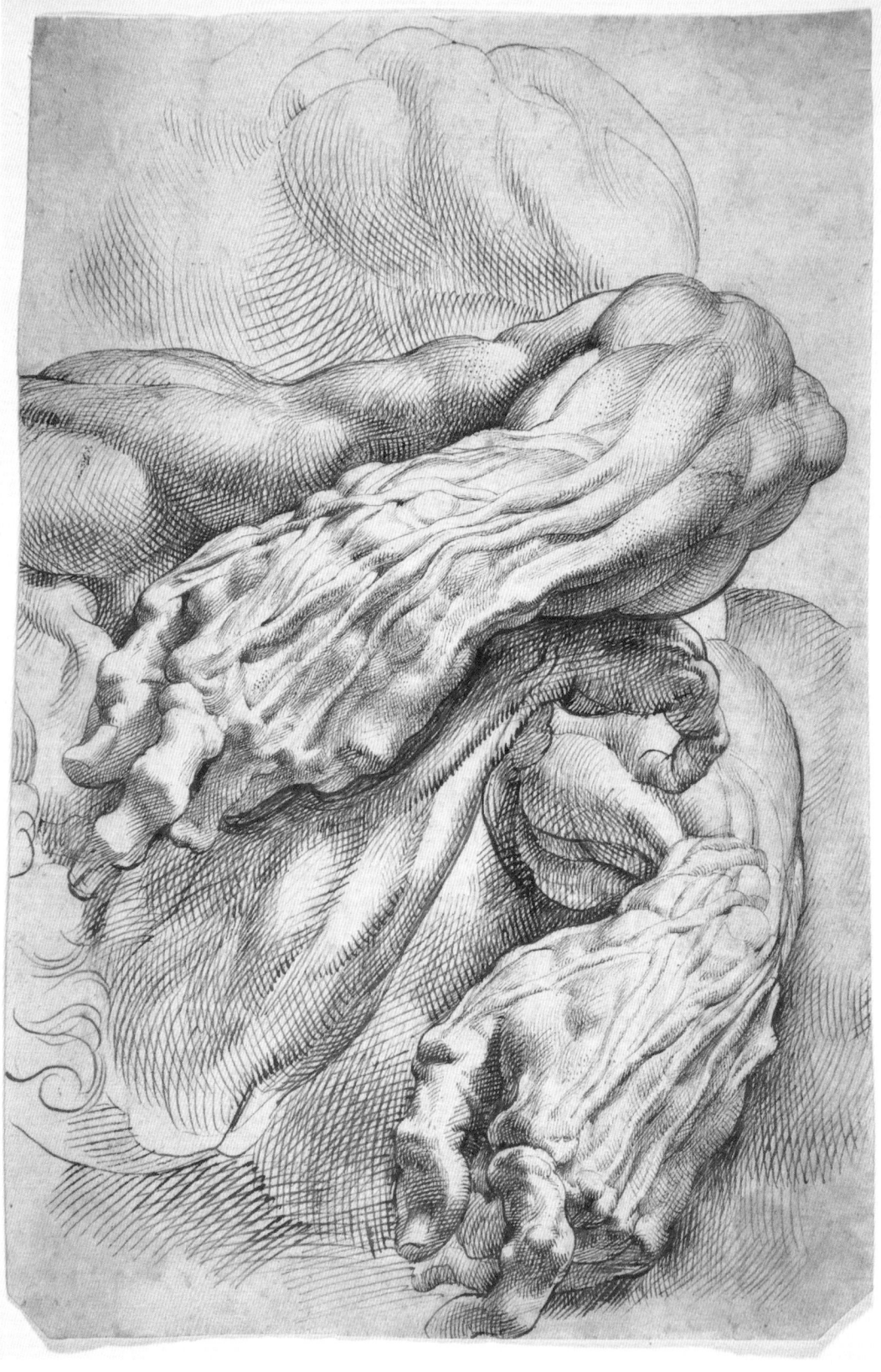

FOUR

HEADS, HANDS, AND FEET

To copy and create seem contradictory concepts. Yet, throughout the centuries, artists were able to shape their own vision, however innovative or personal, only by absorbing the past.
—EGBERT HAVERKAMP-BEGEMANN, *CREATIVE COPIES*

Well-rounded figure-drawing instruction centers on two approaches: conceptual (informing the mind) and observational (training the eye). A conceptual approach is concerned with understanding structure, anatomy, and proportion. We can draw a believable figure, in the ideal, without looking at a model if we understand the mechanics. The other approach is observational drawing: sketching only what you see, not focusing on what is under the skin but on what makes this figure unlike any other. This naturalistic approach trains the eye to site angles, shapes, and value to celebrate one individual, exactly as he is. Both the strength of structure and the sensitivity of nuanced observation are inseparable when one is creating a powerful drawing.

This book draws from both traditions, starting with general principles such as lines of action and movement, siting angles, and modeling form. We face the same struggle as artists before us as we balance our search for universal principles with direct observation to make new art for our times.

In principle, a drawing is always approached as a whole, never as a series of parts; we don't use a formula for drawing different subject matter. The way we draw a head is the same way we approach an apple or a teapot. However, it can be intimidating to draw certain parts of the body because they are detailed, complex, yet familiar. It takes only a small mistake for them to appear wrong. In this chapter, we'll look mostly at three parts of the figure that often intimidate new artists—heads, hands, and feet—and overcome some of our fears by simplifying and practicing.

OPPOSITE: Peter Paul Rubens, *Anatomical Studies: A Left Forearm in Two Positions and a Right Forearm*, ca. 1600–5, pen and brown ink on paper, 10 15/16 x 7 5/16 inches (27.8 x 18.6 cm), Metropolitan Museum of Art, New York

Drawing parts of the body

Here and on the following pages, re-create the drawings on the blank pages provided. As always, work from beginning block-in lines to smaller shapes.

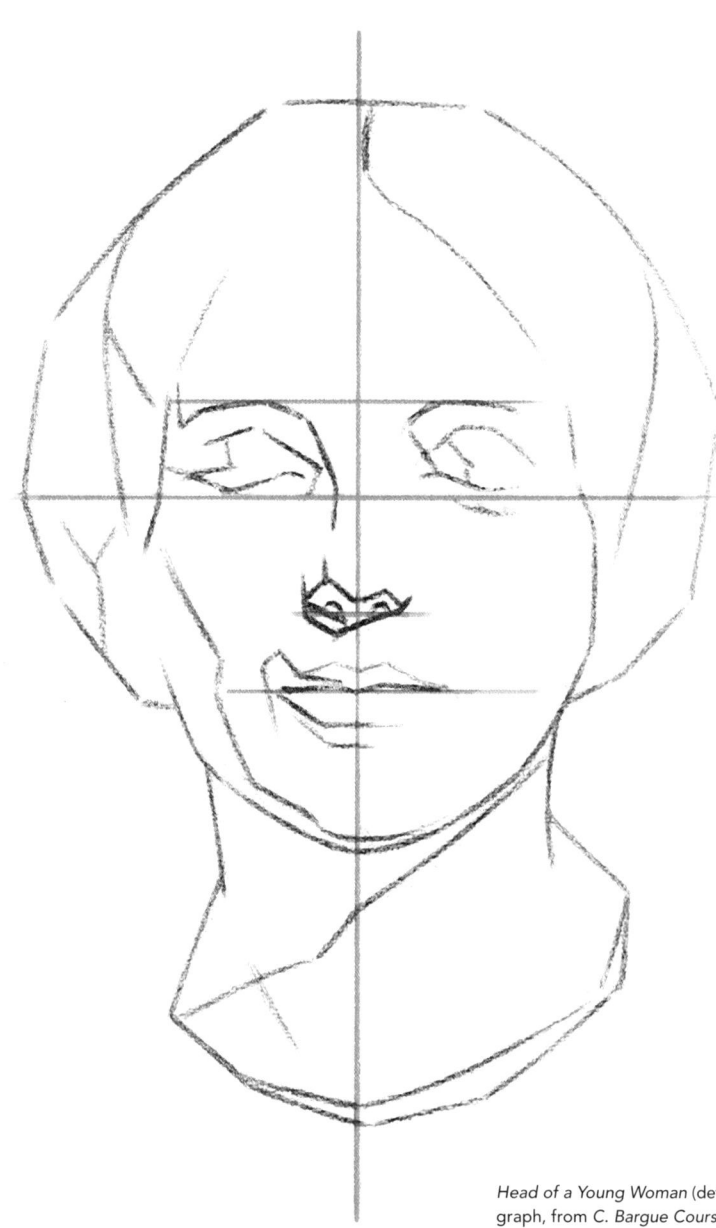

Head of a Young Woman (detail), lithograph, from *C. Bargue Cours de dessin*, published ca. 1866–71. Image courtesy of the Art Renewal Center

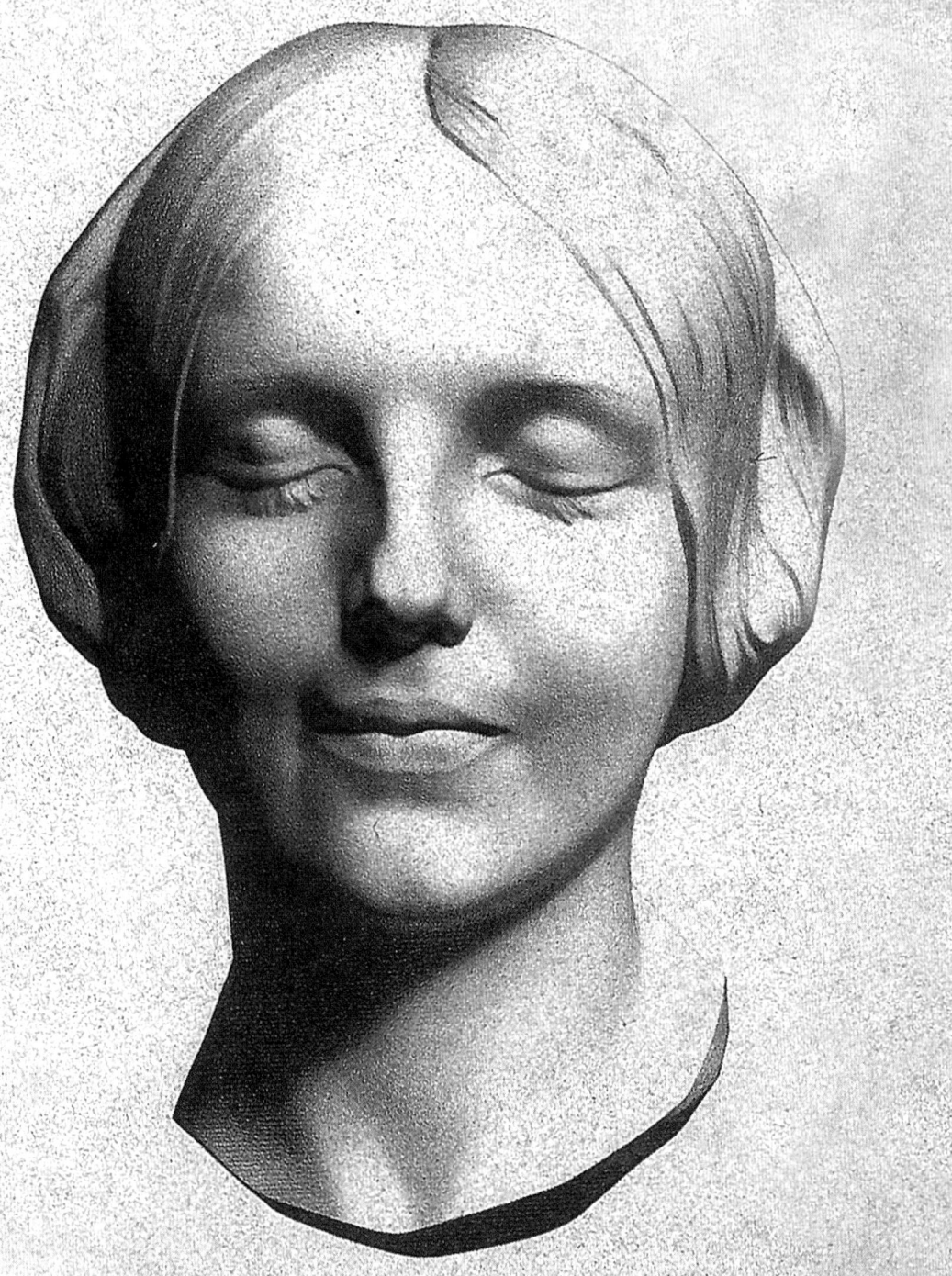

Anyone interested can still work through the Bargue plates today, thanks to a reprinting of *The Charles Bargue and Jean-Léon Gérôme Drawing Course*, by Gerald M. Ackerman and Graydon Parrish.

Head of a Young Woman (detail), lithograph, from *C. Bargue Cours de dessin*, published ca. 1866–71. Image courtesy of the Art Renewal Center

Use the block in provided as a chance to practice your shading. See pages 94–95 for another example.

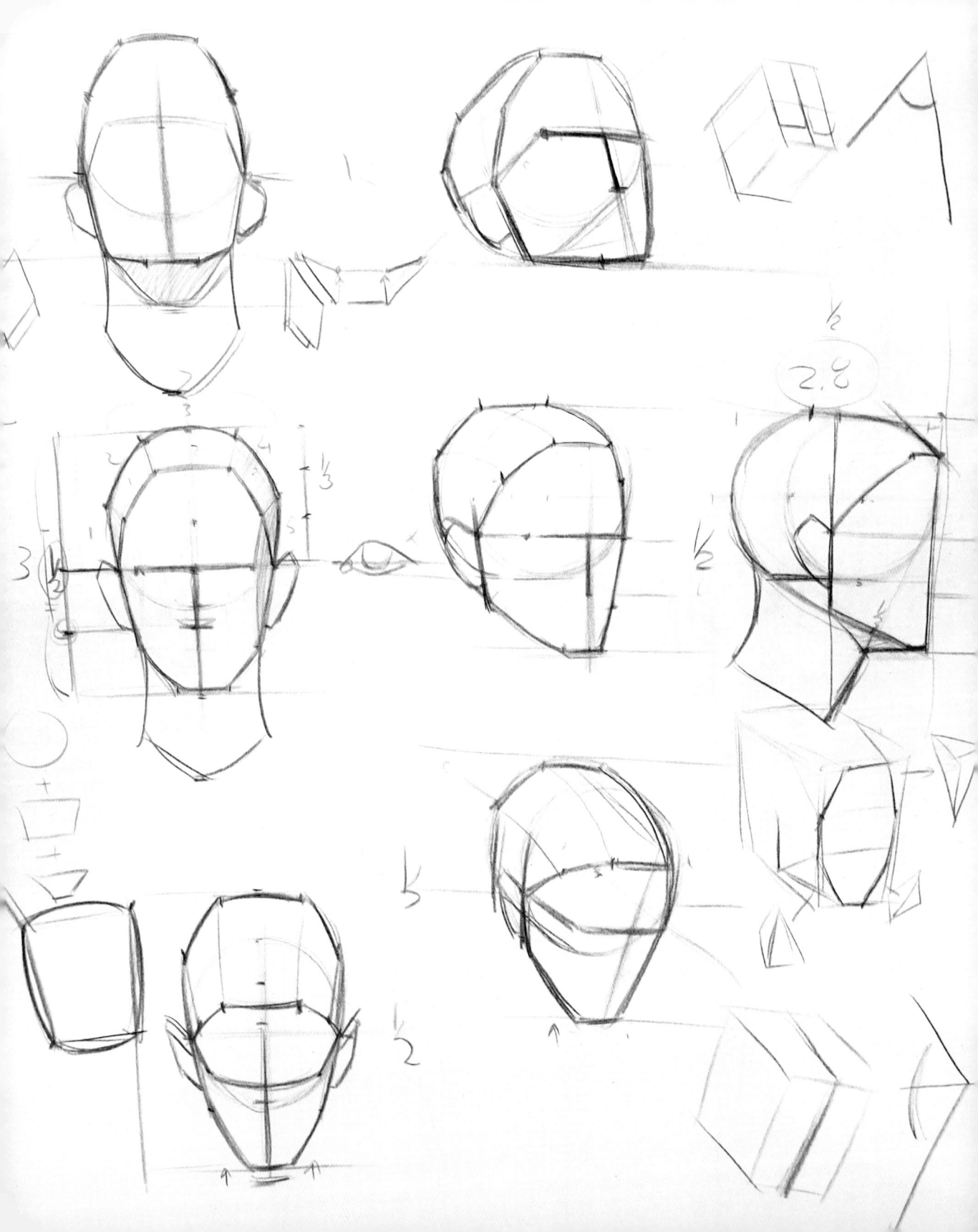

Kevin Chen, *Head Lay-in Demonstration*, 2017, graphite pencil on newsprint, 24 x 18 inches (61 x 45.7 cm), Analytical Figure Drawing class. Image courtesy of ConceptDesignAcad.com

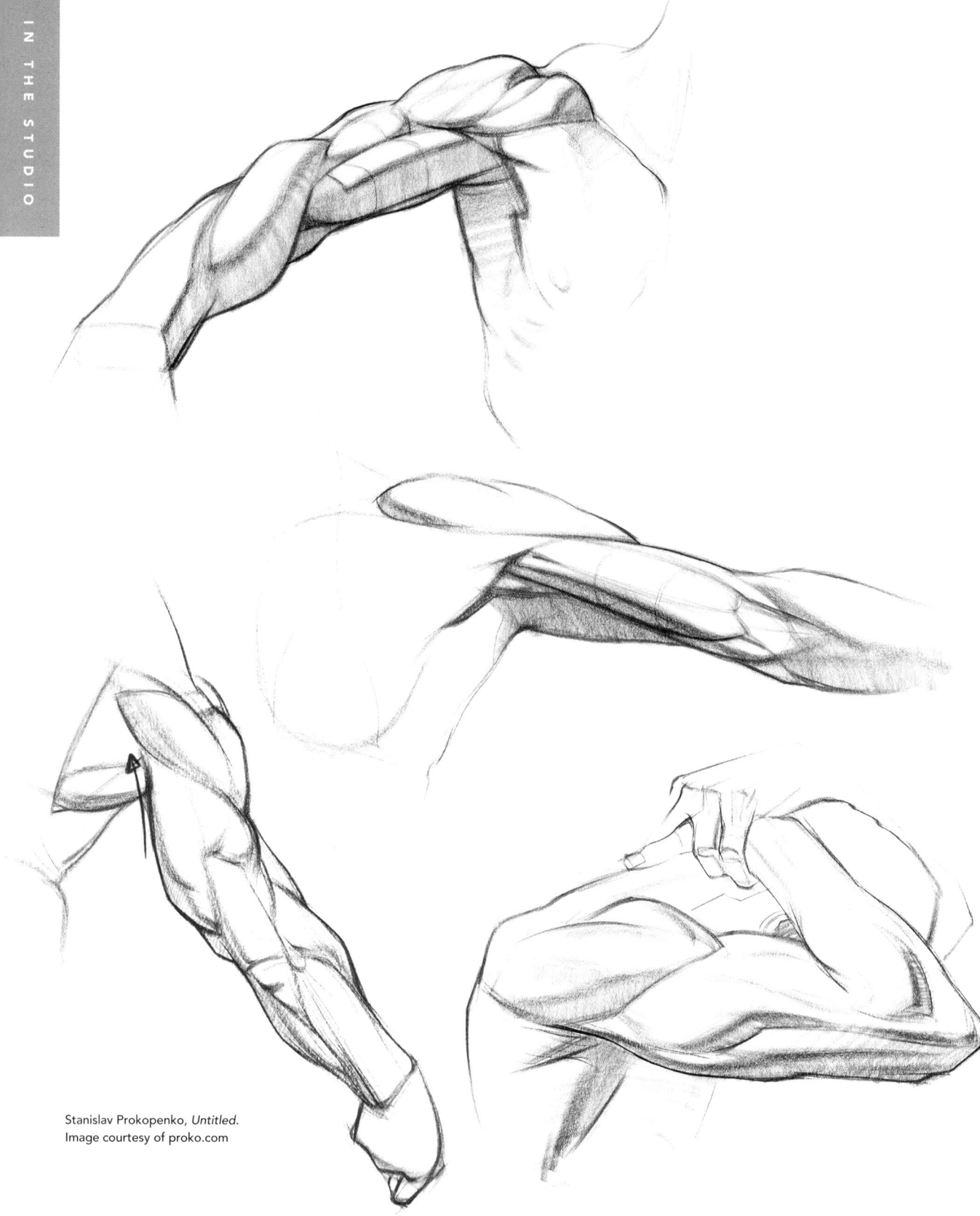

Stanislav Prokopenko, *Untitled*.
Image courtesy of proko.com

Stanislav Prokopenko, *Untitled*.
Image courtesy of proko.com

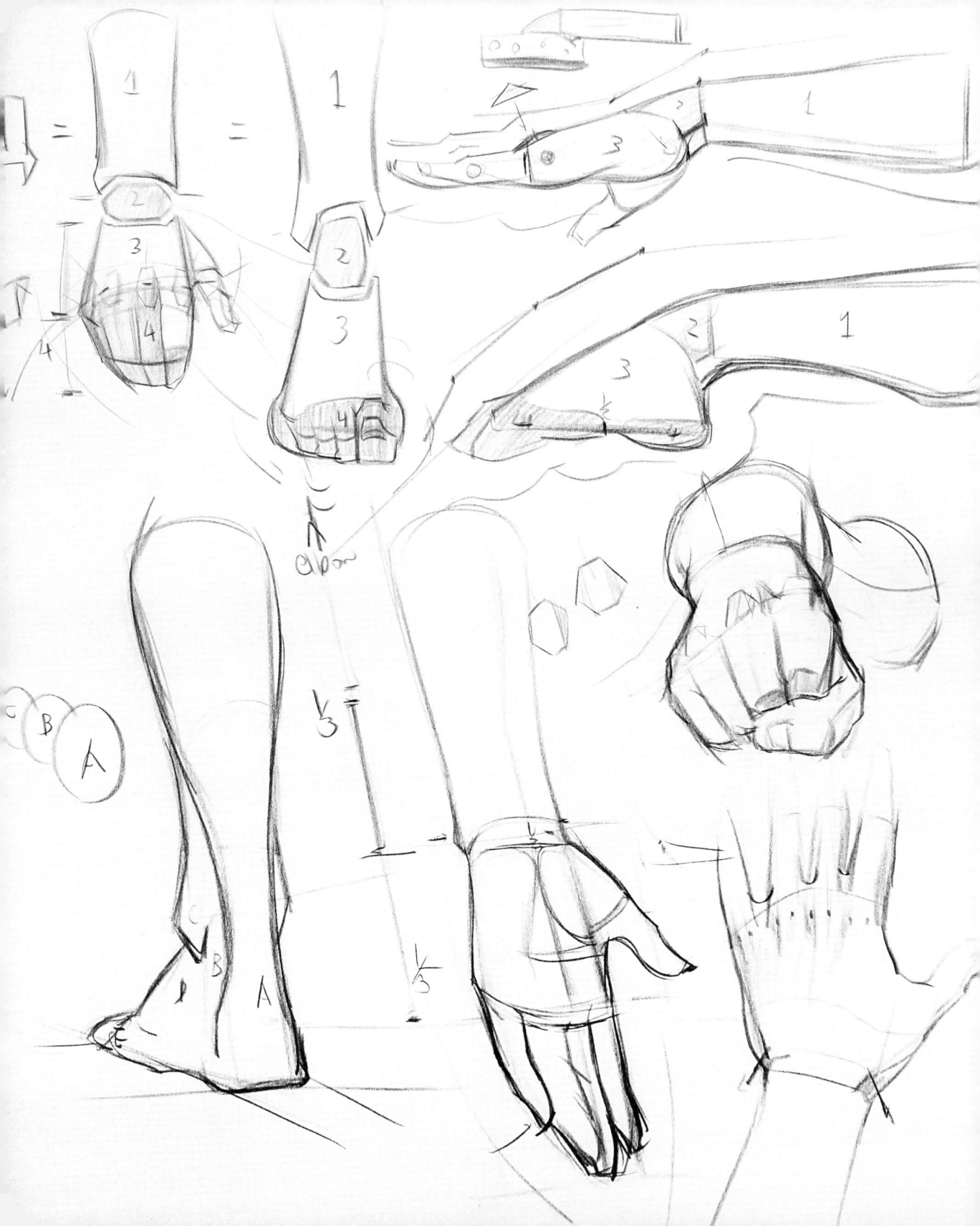

Kevin Chen, *Hands and Feet*, 2017, graphite pencil on newsprint, 24 x 18 inches (61 x 45.7 cm), Analytical Figure Drawing class. Image courtesy of ConceptDesignAcad.com

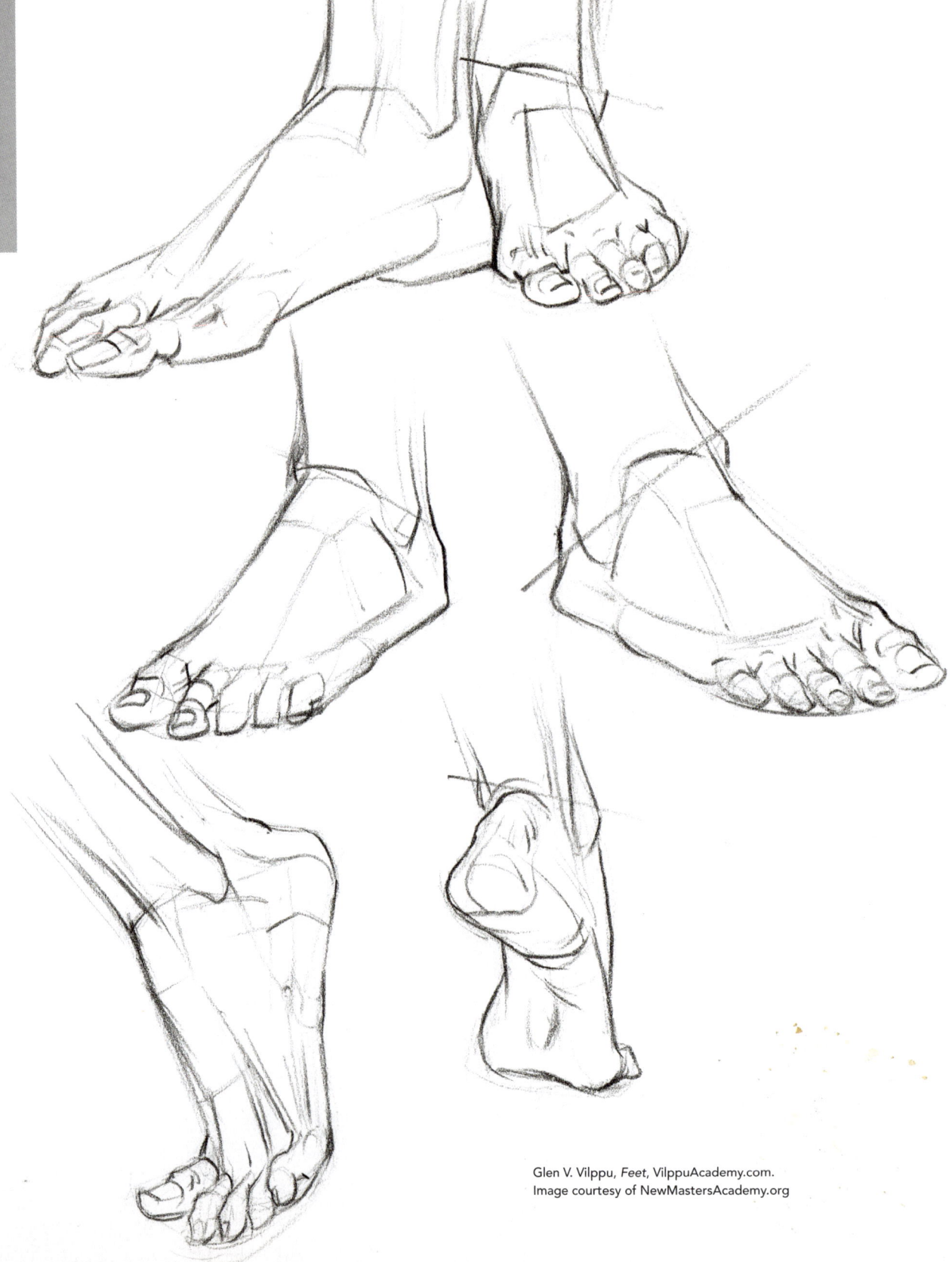

Glen V. Vilppu, *Feet*, VilppuAcademy.com.
Image courtesy of NewMastersAcademy.org

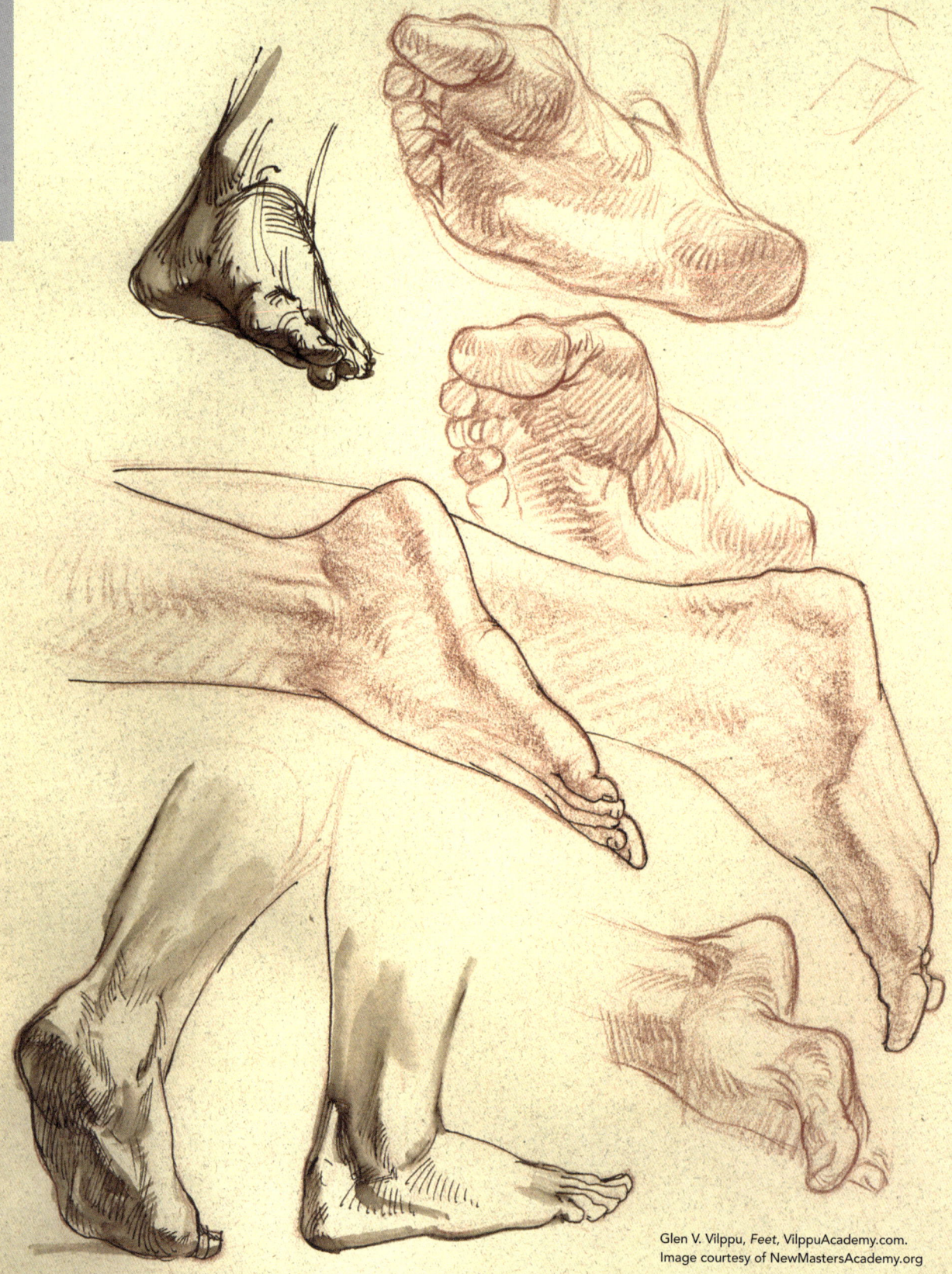

Glen V. Vilppu, *Feet*, VilppuAcademy.com.
Image courtesy of NewMastersAcademy.org

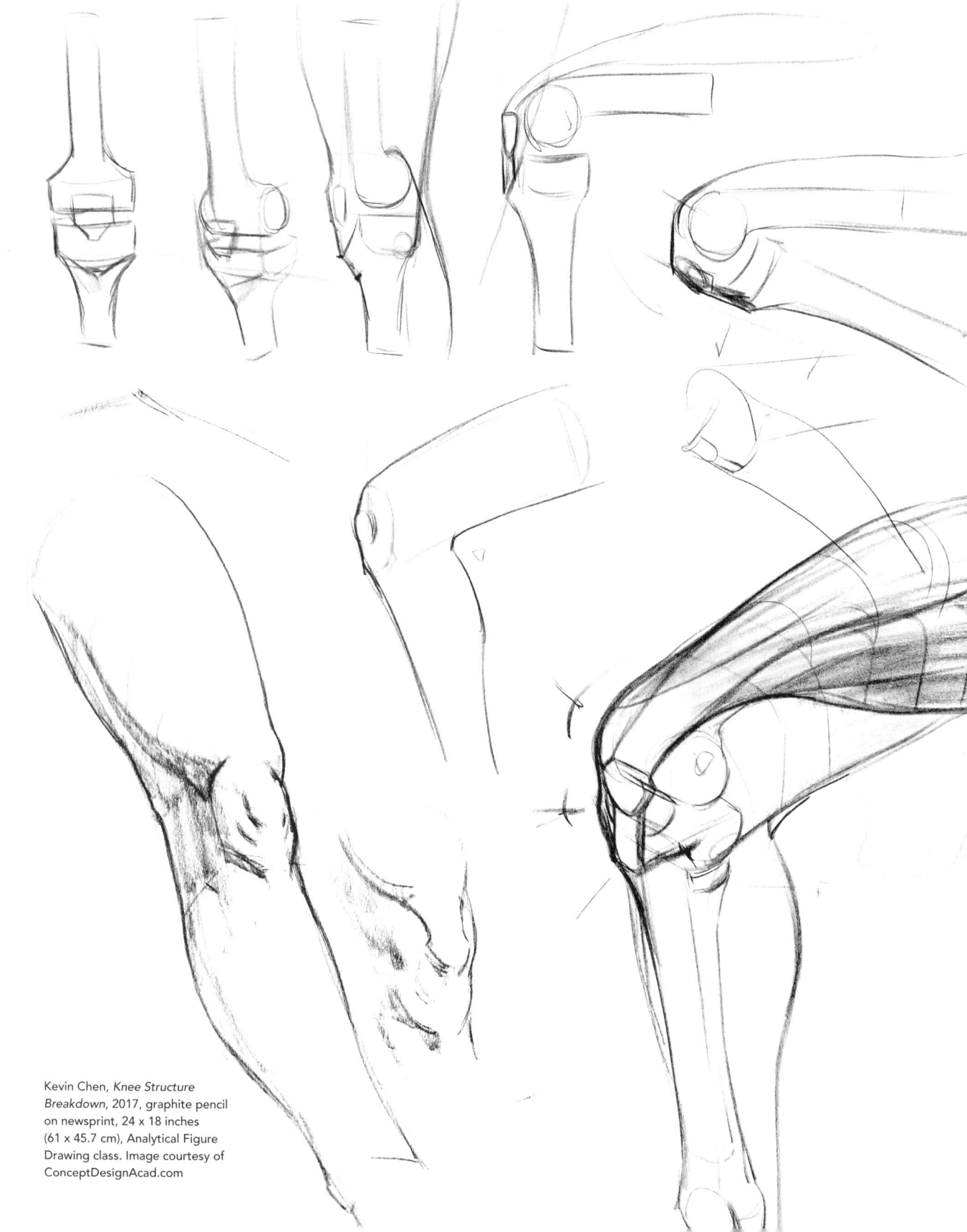

Kevin Chen, *Knee Structure Breakdown*, 2017, graphite pencil on newsprint, 24 x 18 inches (61 x 45.7 cm), Analytical Figure Drawing class. Image courtesy of ConceptDesignAcad.com

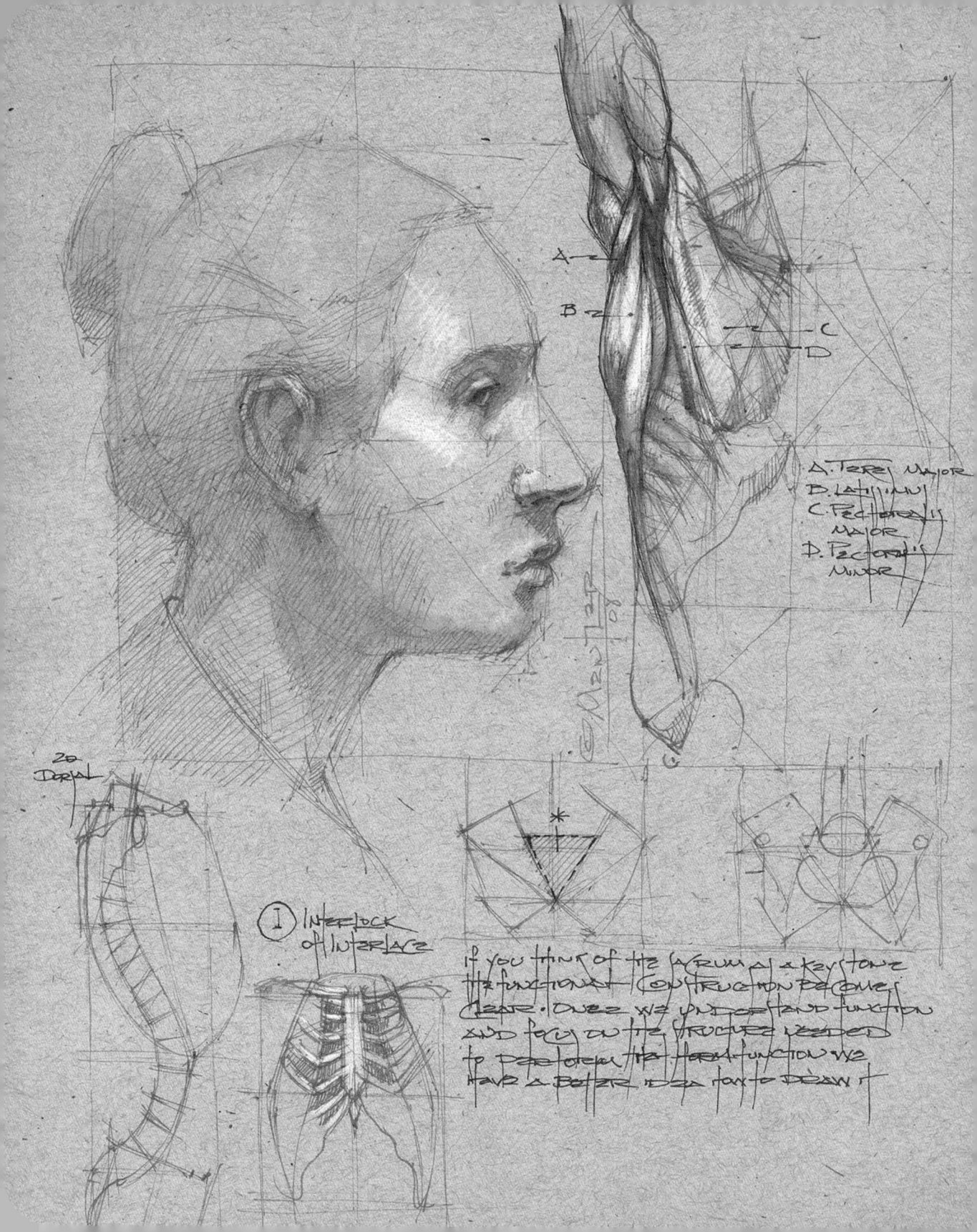

A –
B –
– C
– D

A. Terei Major
B. Latissimus
C. Pectoralis
   Major.
D. Pectoralis
   Minor

2o Dorsal

① Interlock
   or Interlace

If you think of the sacrum as a keystone the functional construction becomes clear. Once we understand function and focus on the structure needed to perform the desired function we have a better idea how to draw it

Michael Mentler, *From the Sketchbook*, 2007, ink wash, pen, and gouache heightened with white, 12 x 9 inches (30.5 x 22.9 cm)

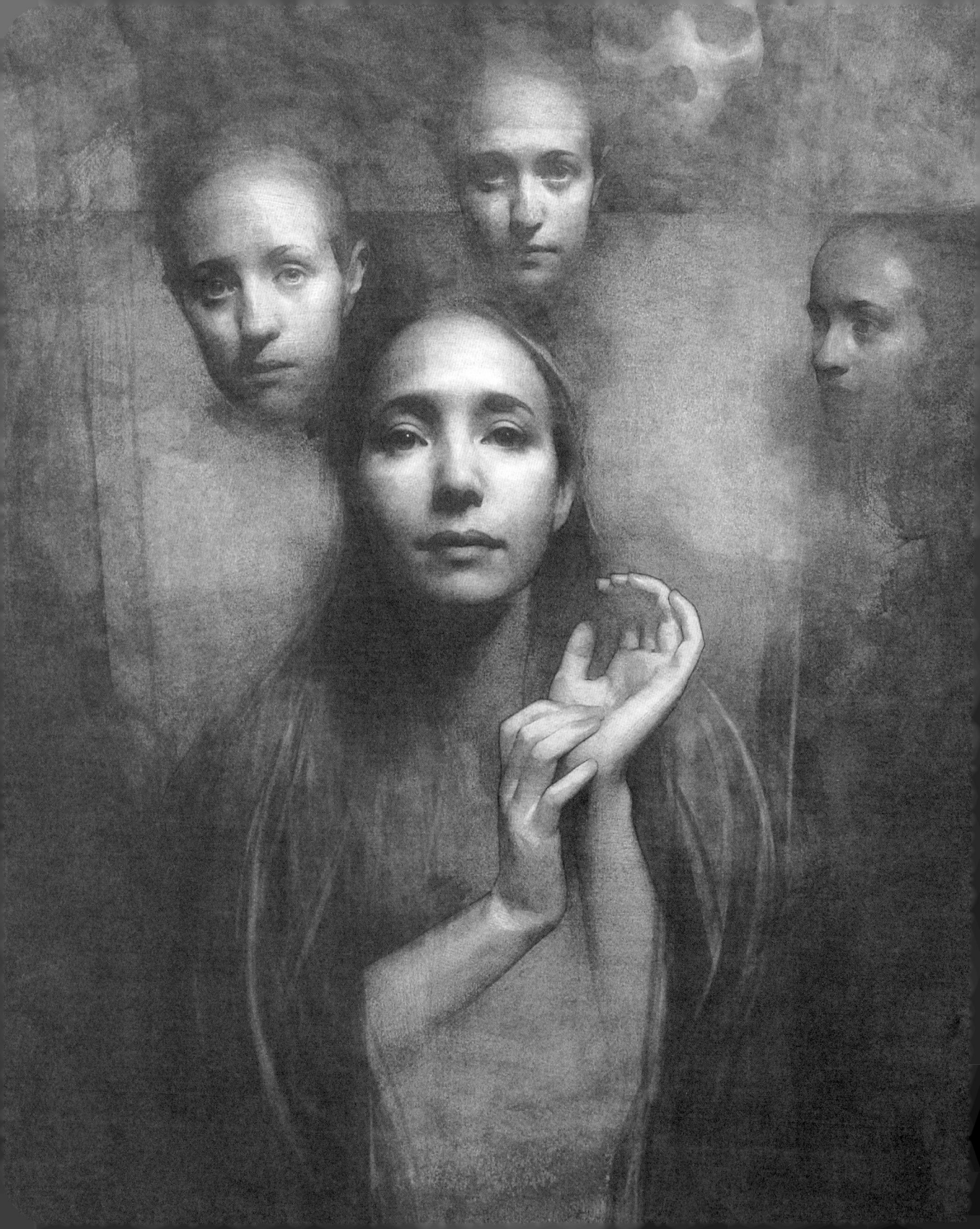

FIVE

VALUE AND FORM

Then come close to Nature. Then, as if no one had ever tried before,
try to say what you see and feel and love and lose.
—RAINER MARIA RILKE, *LETTERS TO A YOUNG POET*

Light and darkness separate day from night, creating rhythms for our lives so foundational that we scarcely think of them. Light is revealing, making our surroundings visible, solid, and volumetric, while darkness is shadowed and hidden. Both are essential in art, for without contrast there is nothing to see.

In the first four chapters of the book we focused on line, shape, and volume; now we move on to *tone*, or *value*. Value is the range of darkness or lightness seen in the visible world, such as in a black-and-white photograph. In this stage of the drawing, we separate our objects into light and dark and decide on the value of our background (if there is one).

Any object hit by light has three main components: light, shadow, and halftones. We'll start by focusing only on light and shadow. Eventually we'll turn to halftones—detailed areas of form that gradate from dark to light—but first we need to consider the image as a whole, grouping it into large shapes of light and shadow that will provide a blueprint for the next stage of the drawing.

One of the biggest challenges facing new draftsmen is simplifying all the details we see in life into a cohesive image. Often beginners are unsure what is important, and so they include unnecessary details that weaken the design. A study of value helps you gain confidence when editing life into art. A masterful handling of value helps you use tones as a compositional device, setting the mood of the work, guiding the eye through the picture—rather than just copying what you see.

OPPOSITE: Stephen Bauman, *Other Voices*, 2015, graphite on paper, 24 x 18 inches (61 x 45.7 cm), private collection

Mapping value

In art when starting, we work from general to specific and from large ideas to smaller ones. In Chapter 1, we start with action lines that describe only the broadest movements of our model and gradually tighten our work with careful measurements. We now approach our study of tone the same way. We begin with the largest impressions about light or shadow on our model before concerning ourselves with incidental value changes.

The first step is to simplify the many value gradations seen in life into the largest possible separate shapes, like puzzle pieces. Artists group, or "map," values to create a memorable visual statement that captures the viewer's attention from a distance. We start by dividing the picture into two groups: light and darks. The shape of the darks is determined by the boundary of the shadow, called a "core shadow." This is an edge that appears right before the halftone dissolves into shadow. The core shadow should be drawn with as much nuanced accuracy as you can manage. Use predominantly straight lines and go slightly darker with your markings than for the body of the shadow. The goal is to keep your shapes as simple as possible, but the edges as nuanced as possible.

Once you have your shadow shapes mapped, fill them in lightly with flat tone. Rendering the shadow as a flat shape, without a lot of busy specks of light to draw our eye, captures the diaphanous nature of shadows. The shadow carries no visual weight and looks barely there. Later you can add volume by including reflected light, but for now, the slightly darker core shadow suffices to give the shadow luminosity. To see a few examples of mapping value, look at step 5 of John Samuel Agar's *Marquis of Lansdown Herakles* on page 13, step 4 of Tenaya Sims's *Holger* on page 15, or Harold Speed's demonstration drawing on page 37.

By this point, you should begin to glimpse how your finished drawing will look. This is also a good time to double-check the accuracy of your drawing before starting to finish. Tiny changes can make big improvements in accuracy. Stand back and flick your eyes back and forth between your drawing and the subject to see if each shadow shape looks exactly right before moving on to the next stage.

OPPOSITE: Juliette Aristides, *Isa*, 2017, charcoal on toned paper, 24 x 18 inches (61 x 45.7 cm)

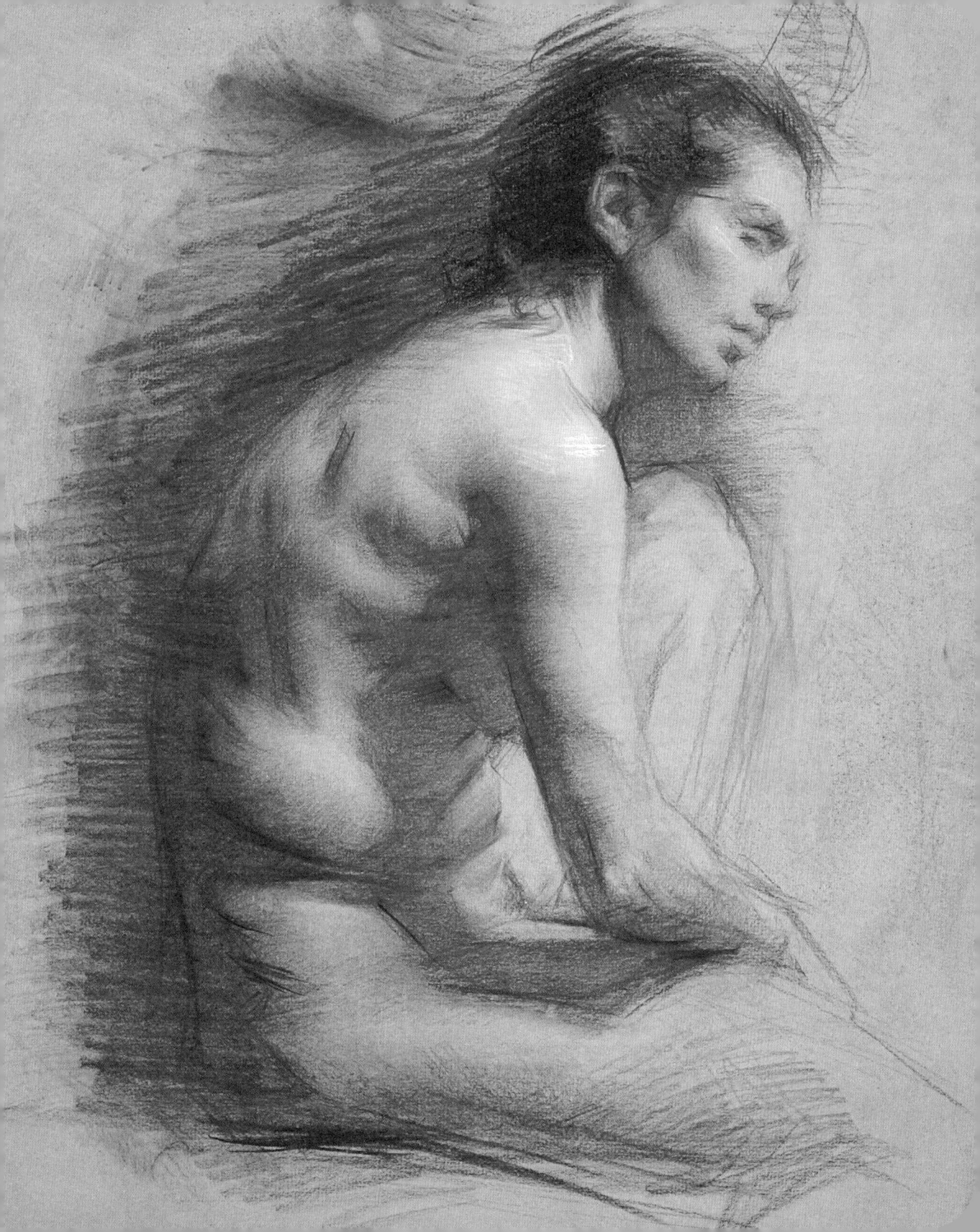

Tone the shadow shapes

Provided are simple outlines of the shadow shapes in Ephraim Rubenstein's *Sara XXI* and *Sara XXIII*, below and opposite. Use washes of tone to build up the flat shadow shapes. Once you have lightly toned the darks, feel free to further render the tone, pushing a few of the darks and finding more specific shapes.

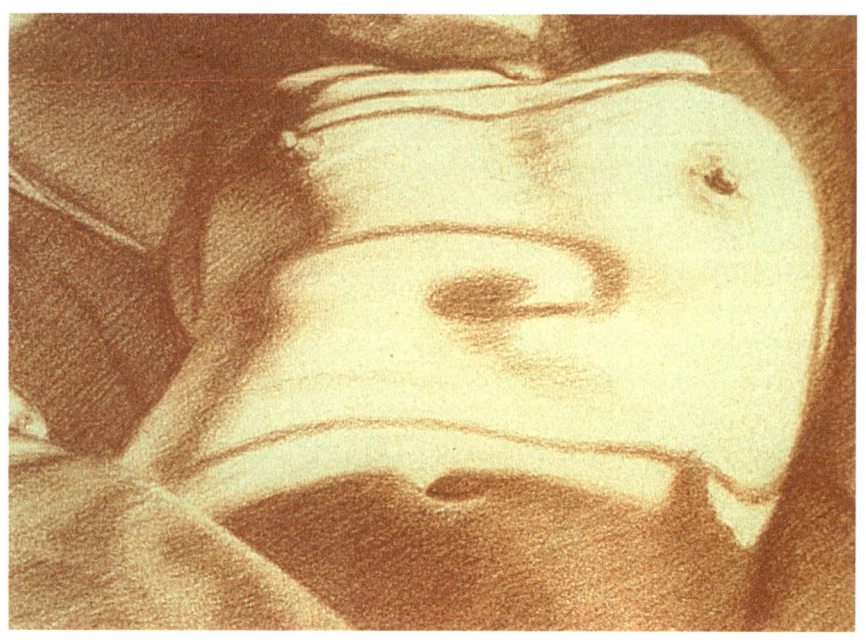

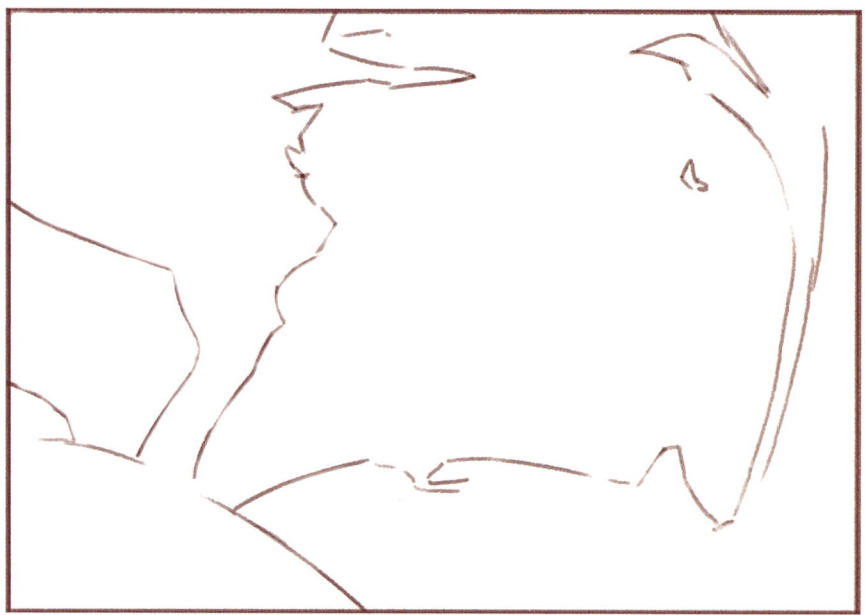

OPPOSITE: Ephraim Rubenstein, *Sara XXI,* 2000, red chalk on paper, 8 x 12 inches (20.3 x 30.5 cm)

BELOW: Ephraim Rubenstein, *Sara XXIII, 2000,* red chalk on paper, 11 x 14 inches (27.9 x 35.6 cm)

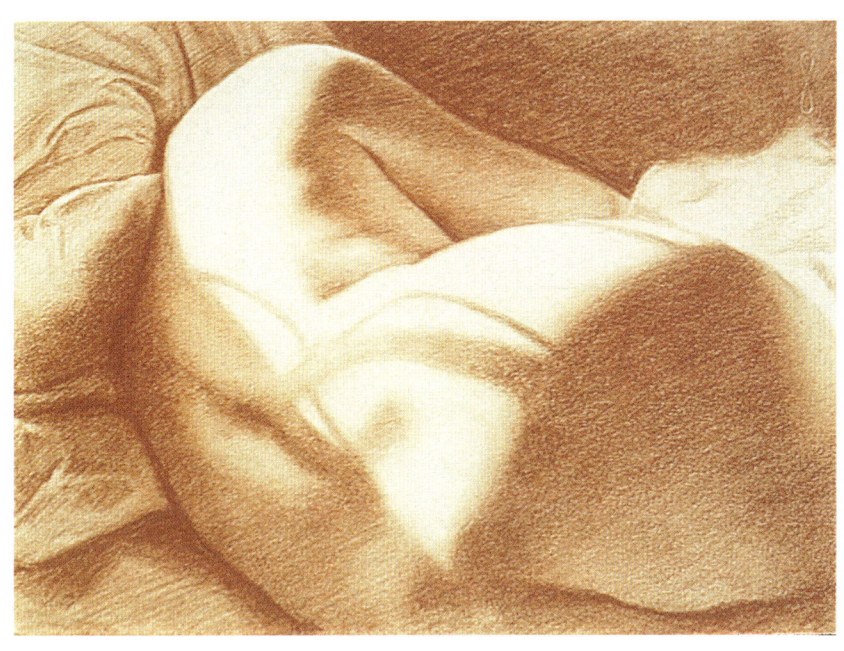

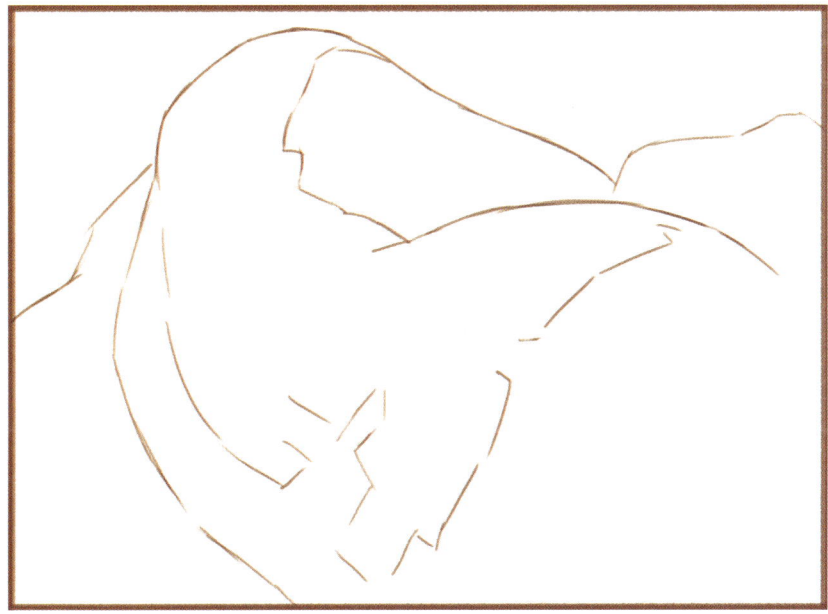

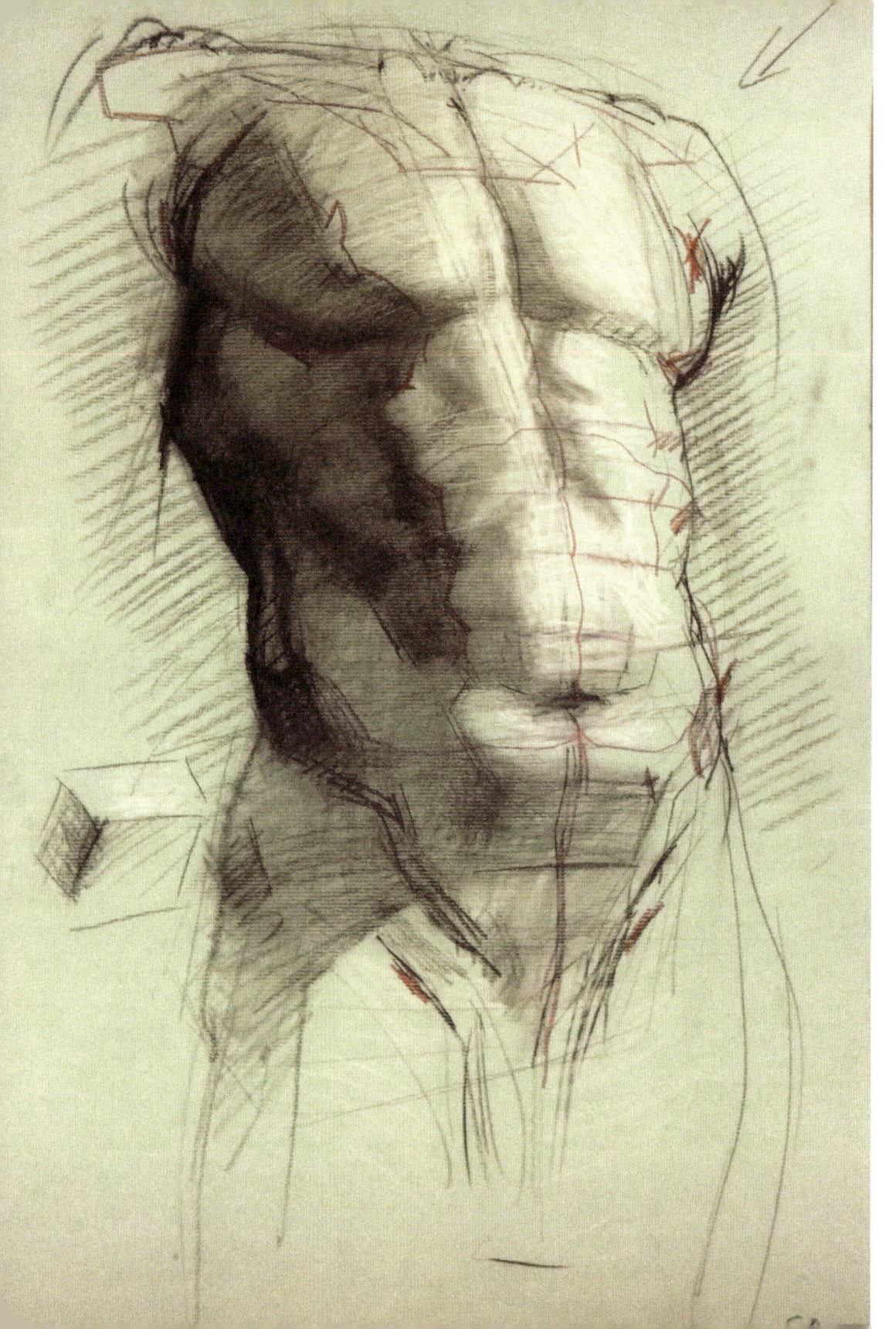

Steven Assael, *Male Torso Study,* 2016, charcoal and chalk on toned paper, 24 x 18 inches (61 x 45.7 cm)

Halftones: the slow art of form drawing

At this point, we have separated the light and shadow into two groups, creating a big impact of light and dark. This contrast makes our image easy to see, yet it doesn't capture the three-dimensionality of the figure. Volume—the feeling of girth, or roundness—comes from small washes of tone placed to show how the skin of the model turns toward the light or dips away from the light into shadow. *Form drawing* is the rendering of halftones that exist between light and shadow. It is the subtle modulation of light over the topography of the human body. For just one example of form drawing, note the subtle changes in tone on the woman's back in Alexey Steele's *The Distant Fire on a Full Moon,* on page 6.

Rendering form is often dismissed as attention to details, yet these tiny idiosyncrasies give the visible world its character and personality. The small forms on the body are not considered details at this stage, but essential aspects of a person, conveying his history and a lifetime of experiences. I may be the last person to ever see this form, under this light, in all of history. To care about these small forms is inseparable from love; we are not caring about people in the abstract but about one person in particular.

If one is in the habit of working without a model—however happy the original conception—one misses those striking effects which the great masters obtained so simply, because they rendered an effect in nature—even a commonplace one—in a naive way.

—EUGÈNE DELACROIX

When I was a student, I spent years doing only quick drawings, the longest pose no more than three hours. I valued energy and movement in a drawing over anything else. Eventually, I became aware that with speed comes the danger of formulaic and repetitious figure drawing. We can end up copying our own style rather than carefully observing nature. The remedy is to slow down and observe more carefully.

The study of form drawing is a careful attention to light hitting your subject. It is impossible to do this both well and quickly. Slow seeing is at the center of artistic creation, and the closer we get to pure observation, the more individual our impressions become. Continually go to nature, study your subject in person, be in the presence of the real thing, and take your time. Likewise, don't rush through an awkward start to your drawing that has lots of mistakes. In the long run, the slow working through of corrections can help make you a better artist. Slow, plodding progress means we are trying to see things for ourselves and are learning rather than just mimicking an effect. Don't rush to adopt an elegant drawing style; be exactly where you are right now and achieve artistic maturity in your own way, in your own time.

Juliette Aristides, *Nina*, 2012, charcoal and sepia on toned paper, 24 x 18 inches (61 x 45.7 cm). Private collection

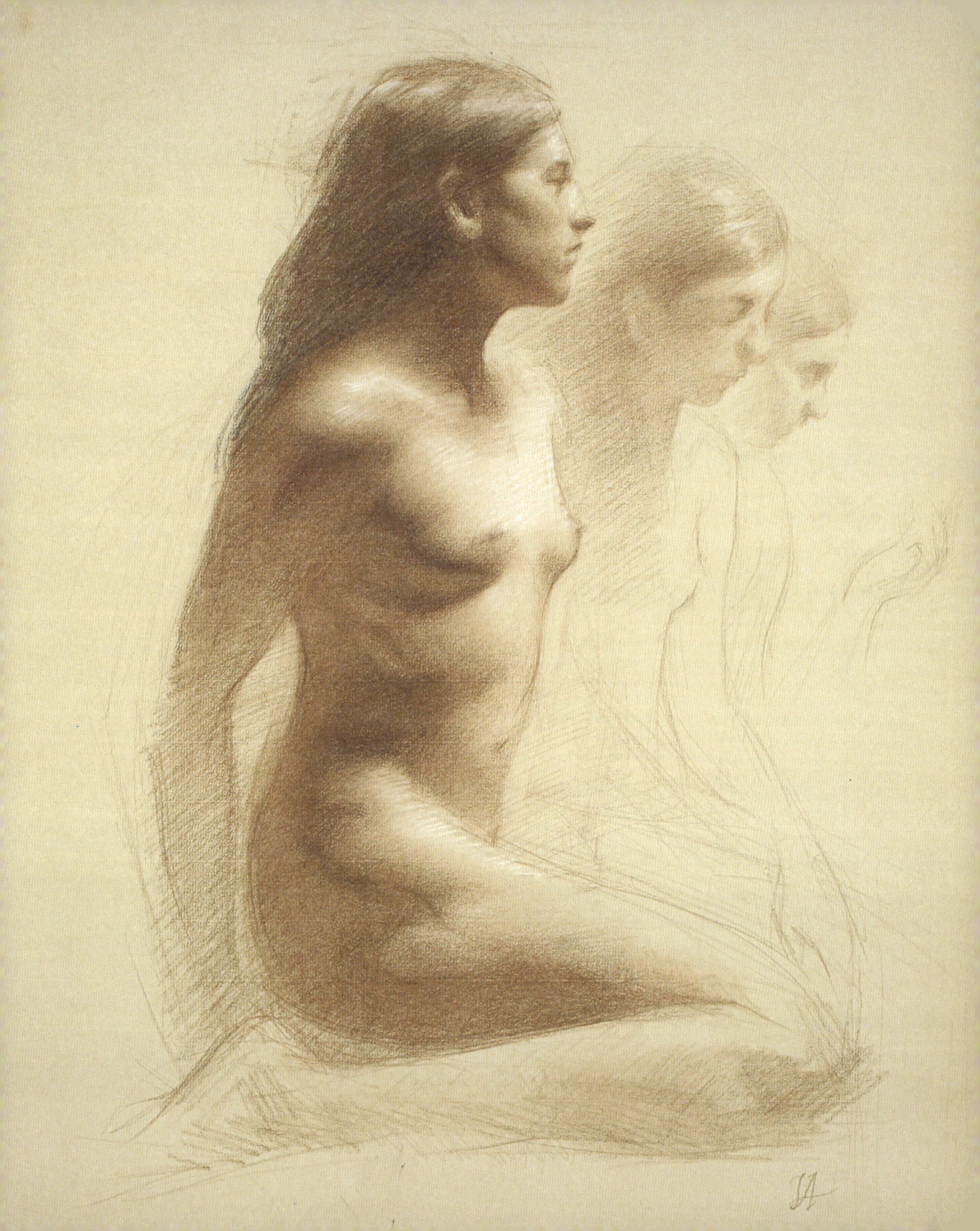

Rendering form

When working from the life model, a beginner's mistake is to forget to put a spotlight on the model and just use whatever random light is already in the room. Choose your light carefully, whether it is from a window or a bulb. Normally, to best reveal form, use only one light source set above and at an angle to your model. Having many light sources or unintentional shadows makes drawing much harder.

In review, the first step is to map the shadow shapes, using predominantly straight lines to clearly define the core shadow. Small changes along the edge of the core shadow indicate plane changes on the surface of the skin, alerting us to look for a value change. Then lightly tone the shadows so they read clearly, like puzzle pieces. Check for any subtle drawing corrections at this point before moving ahead. It's important to add tone only after you think your line drawing is correct. What passes for playful idiosyncrasies in a gesture drawing can look like accidental deformities in a final drawing. The more finished you plan on making your drawing, the more carefully you should begin.

To render form, start by choosing one small, complicated area of the body. It is easier to slow down in an area that is complex than in a large area of broad lights and darks. Starting from the edge of the core shadow, gradually render the form with washes of tone, ending in the light area. You will be tempted to find one tone and use it going down the body in stripes, but choose the more difficult task and render across the form, perpendicular to the shadow edge. Each wash of tone will be like a tiny value step scale, going from dark to light. Try to envision the little areas next to the core shadow as tiny volumes. Your rendering will gradually describe the hills and valleys on the skin as it wraps around muscle, bone, and cartilage.

The tone you put down between your shadow and light may look too dark when first placed on the white of the page, yet may be fine in reality. I remember watching artist Jacob Collins do a demonstration. As he started working, the area of form looked way too dark, but it turned out to be perfect in the context of the completed work. The more halftones, the more volume your drawing will appear to have. The contrast between the darker core shadow and the body of the shadow gives the appearance of ambient reflected light. However, feel free to adjust your shadows to make them lighter if you need more reflected light or specificity in this area.

Form drawing requires us to look deeply and can be a form of meditation. We are not being dazzled or awed with someone else's technical prowess. We absorb our own insights, which come from following a thread of thought slowly over time. This can give you the ability to see *any* particular place on the human form—or on any subject—as unique and worthy of observation.

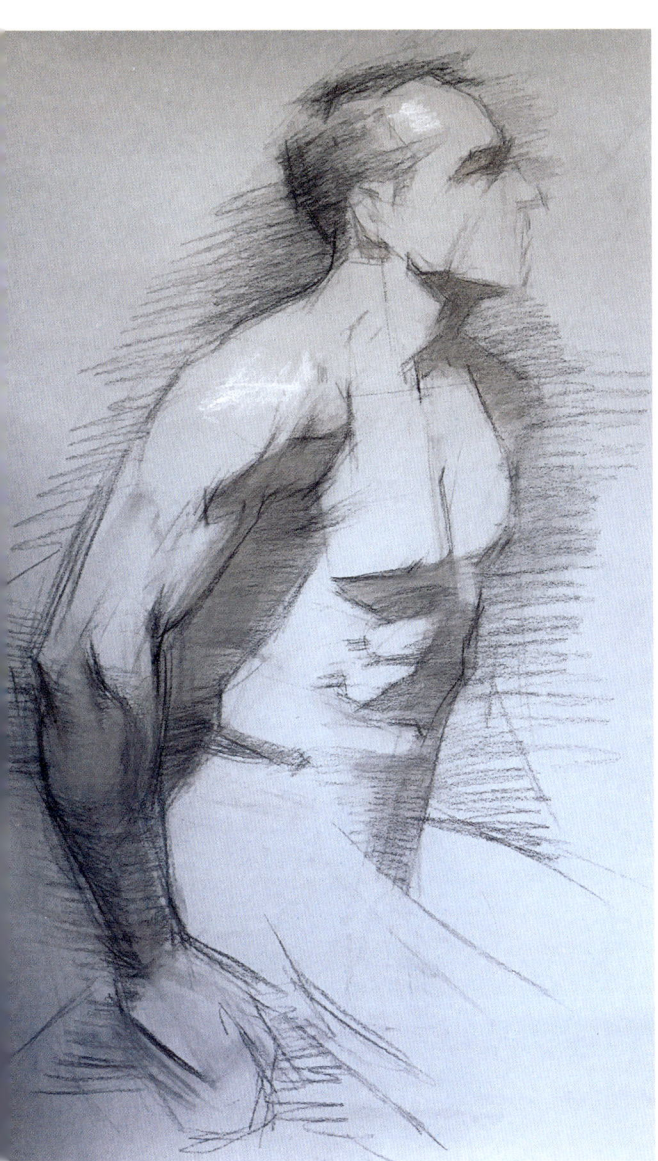
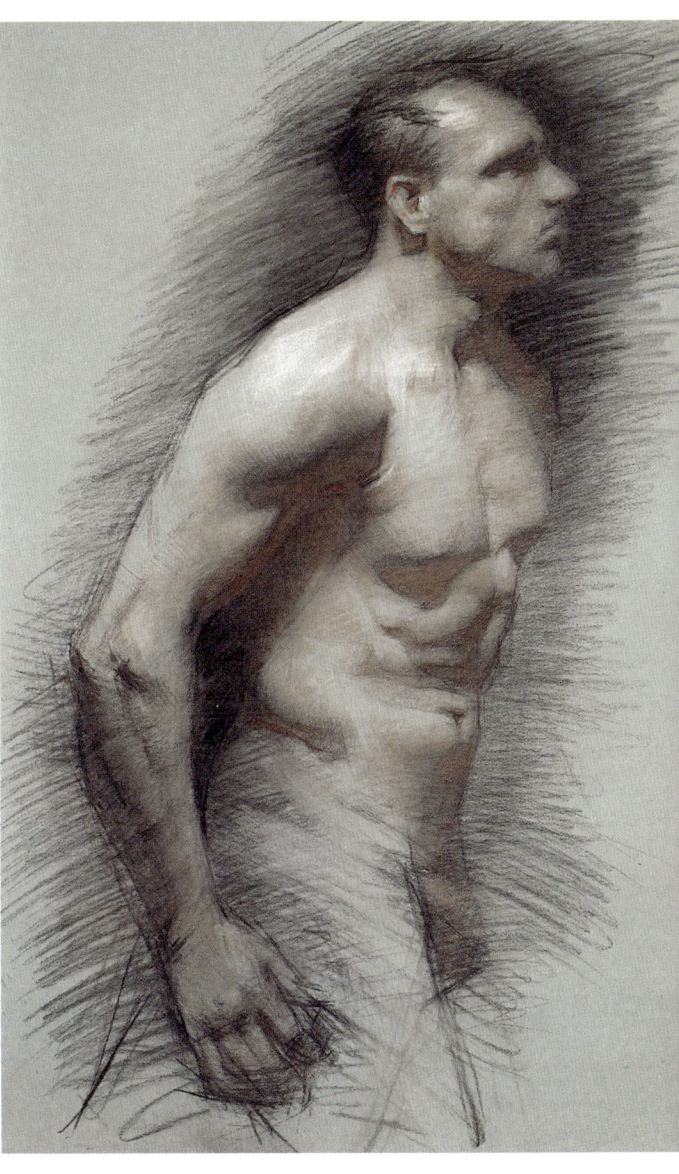

Juliette Aristides, *Eric* (stage one block-in and finished drawing), 2017, charcoal and sepia on toned paper heightened with white, 24 x 18 inches (61 x 45.7 cm)

Form drawing

Finish the partially completed value step scale on the opposite page by matching it to the finished one above it. Then, render the value sphere on the outline provided. Start by lightly toning the shapes. If it looks the way you want it to, push the full value range of the darks in the shadows. To finish, render gradations of tone between the shadow and the light. Feel free to leave the background the white of the page or tone it.

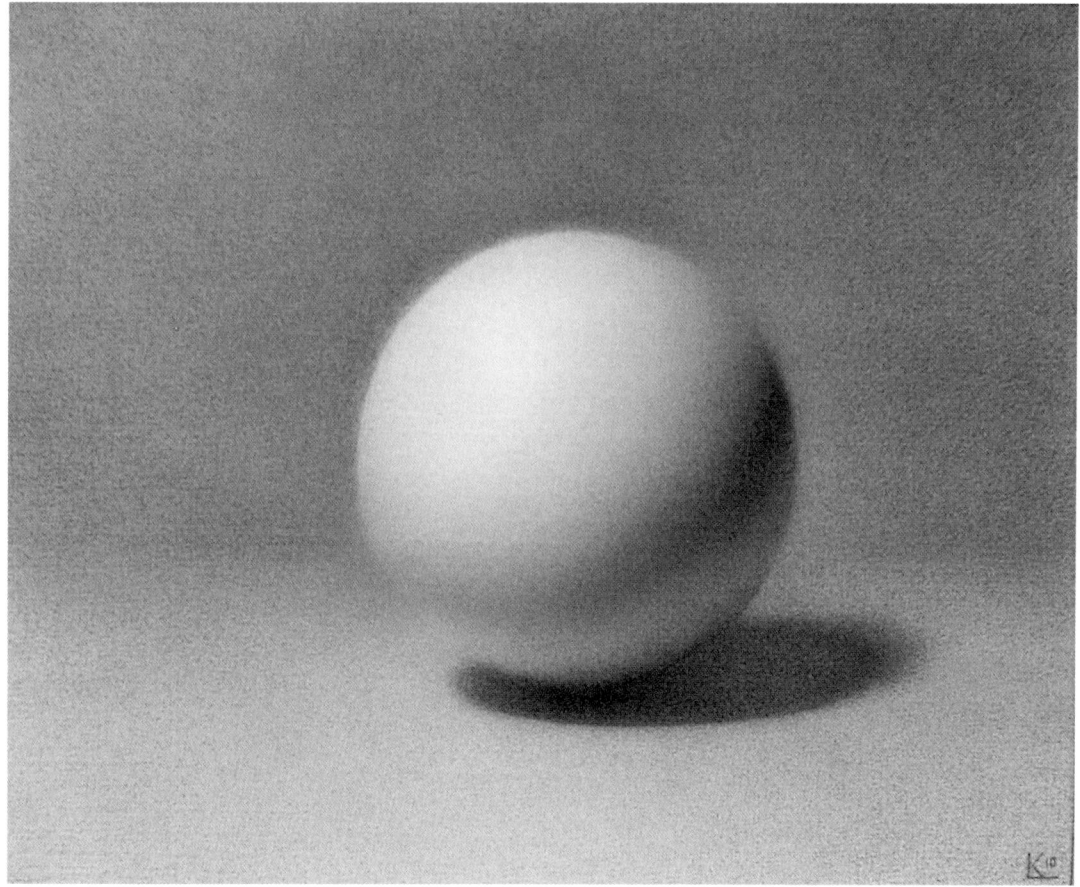

ABOVE: Damien Leeds, *Sphere*, 2010, charcoal on paper, 8 x 10 inches (20.3 x 25.4 cm)

OPPOSITE: A value step scale is a row or column of nine value squares, with white at one end and black at the other. The nine value steps roughly correspond to the stages seen when light hits an object.

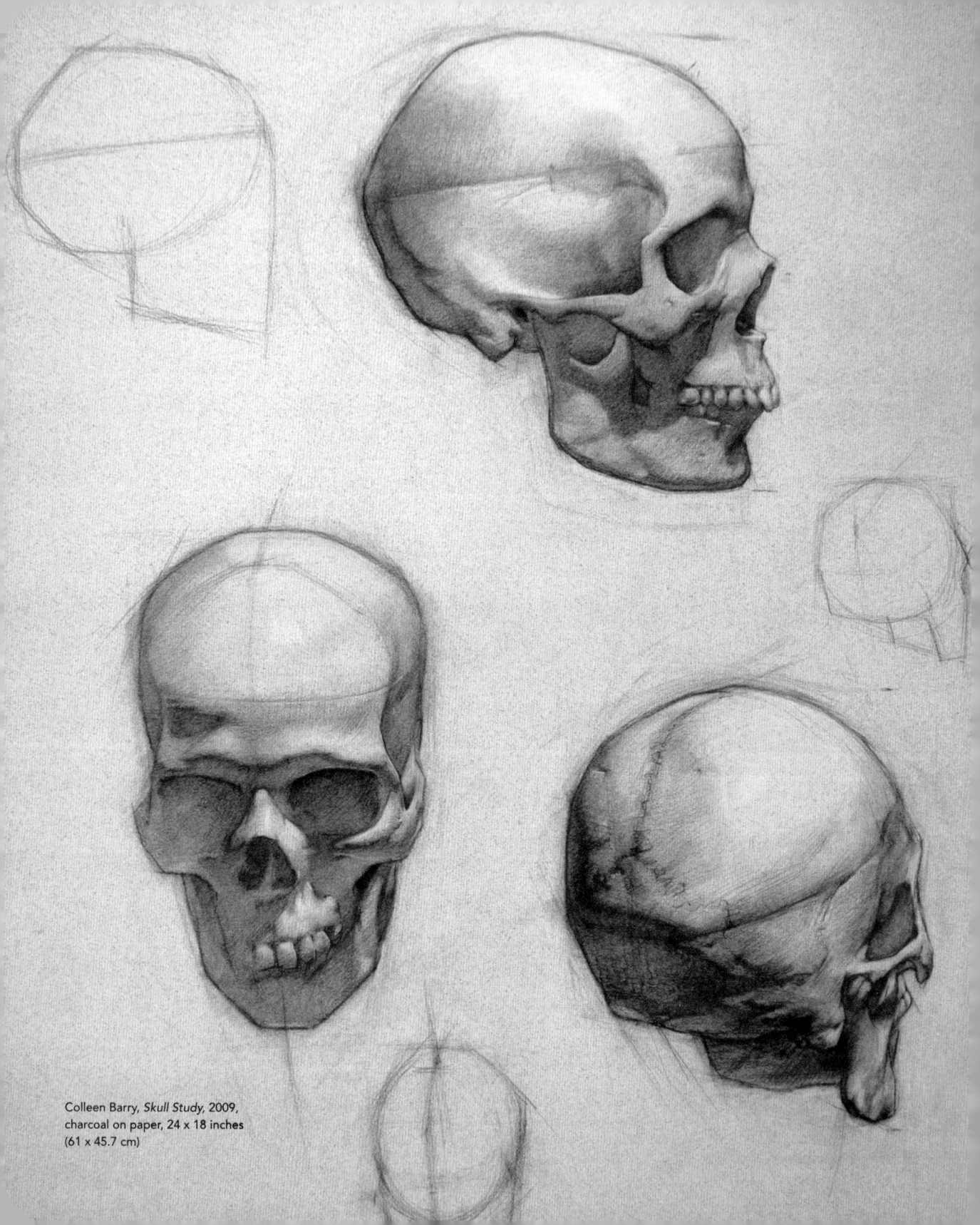

Colleen Barry, *Skull Study*, 2009,
charcoal on paper, 24 x 18 inches
(61 x 45.7 cm)

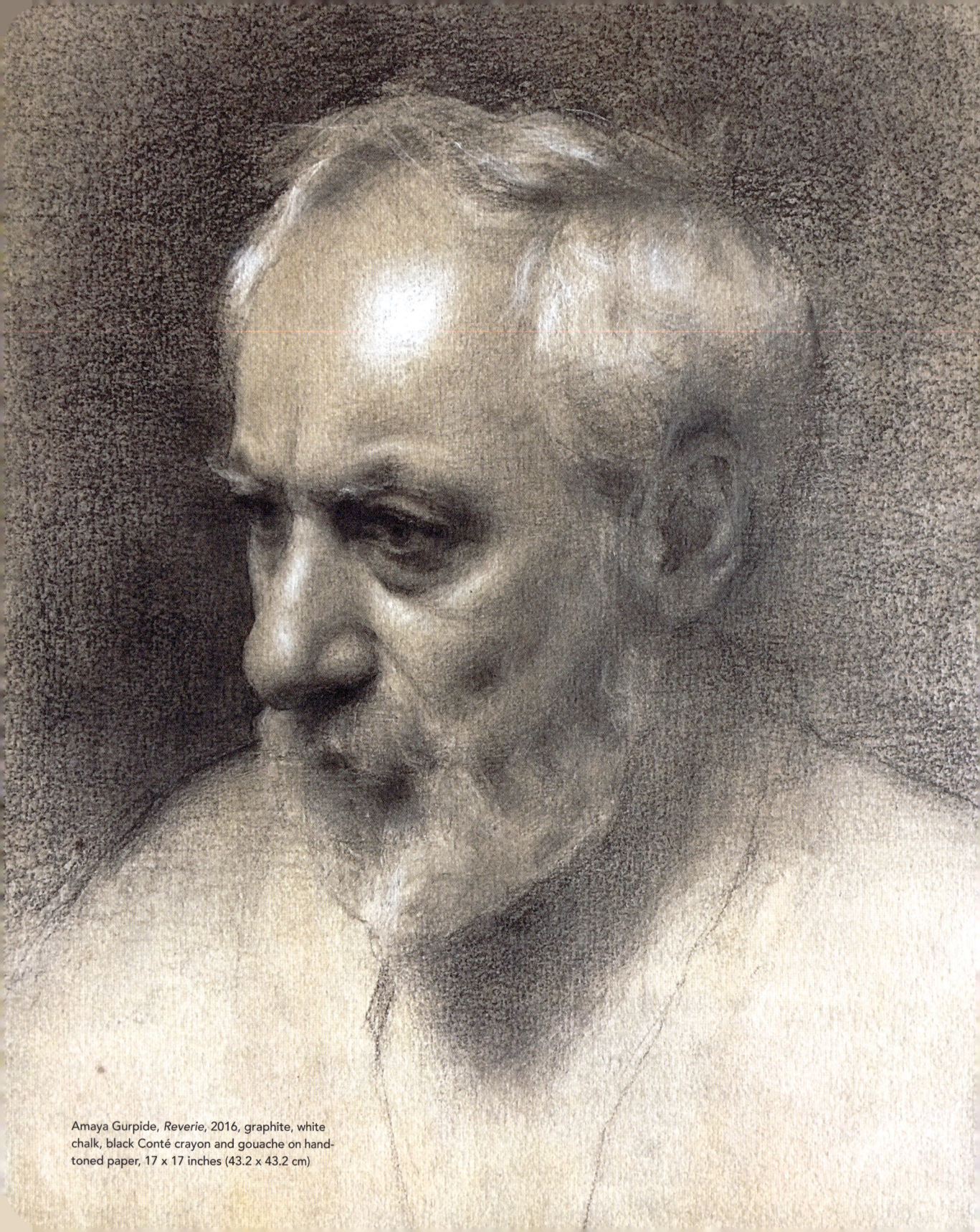

Amaya Gurpide, *Reverie*, 2016, graphite, white chalk, black Conté crayon and gouache on hand-toned paper, 17 x 17 inches (43.2 x 43.2 cm)

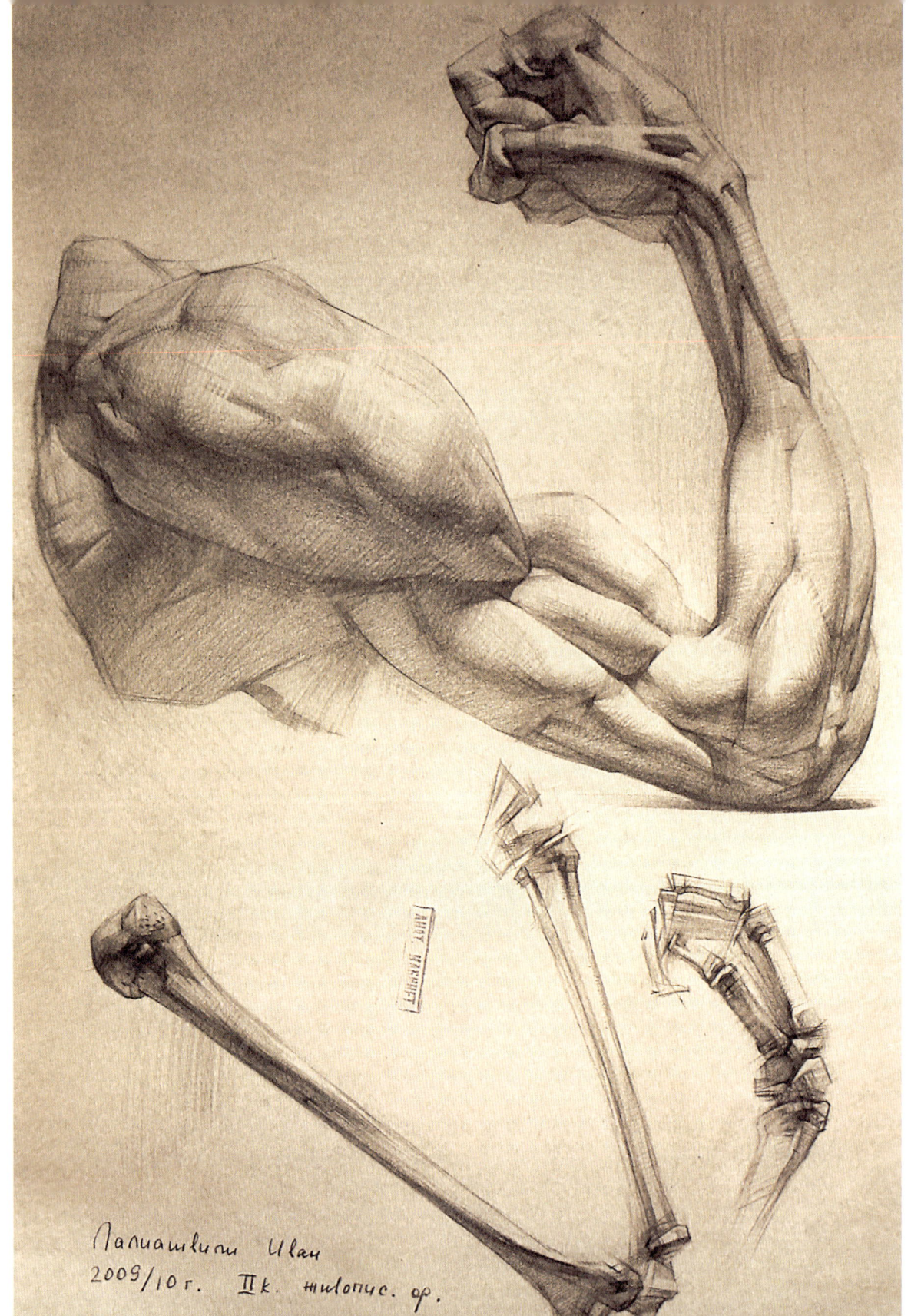

Лапиашвили Иван
2009/10 г. II к. жилопис. ор.

Ivan Laliashvili, Untitled, 2009-10, brown sepia on paper, 19 $\frac{7}{10}$ x 15 $\frac{7}{10}$ inches (50 x 40 cm)

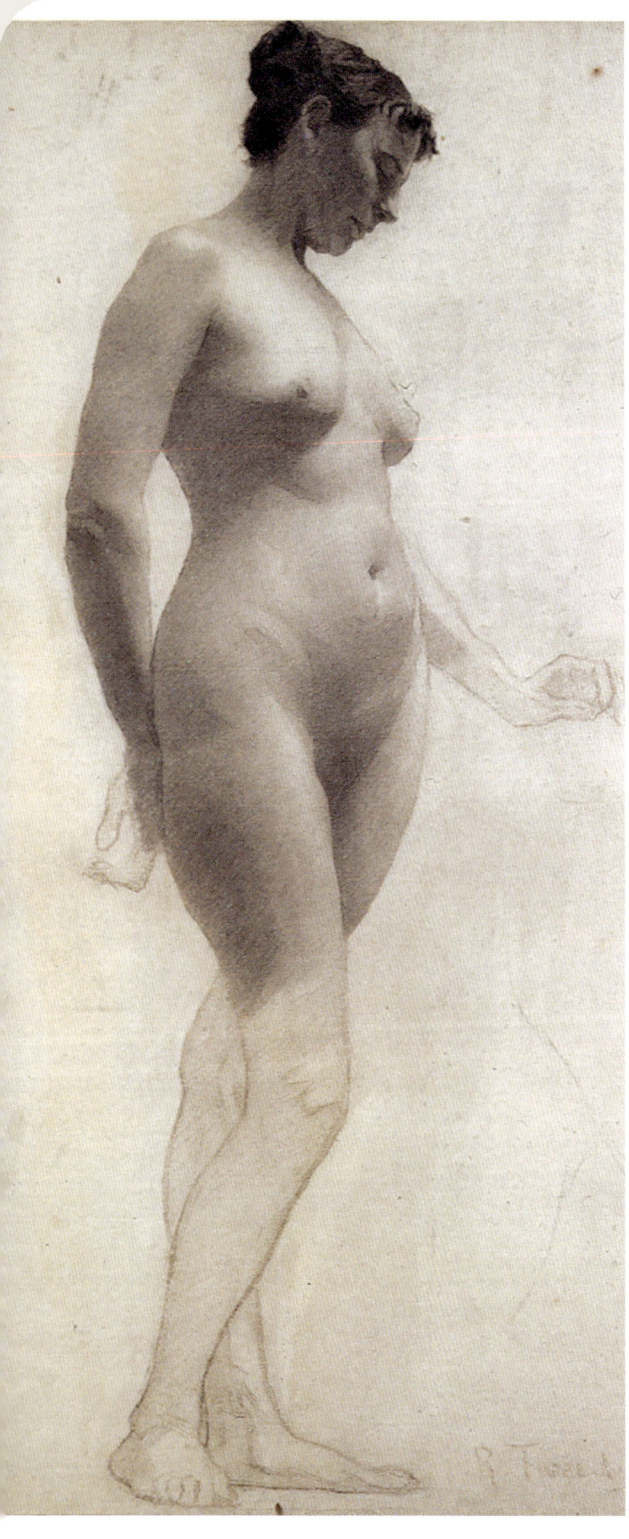

Richard Tweedy, *Untitled* (academic drawing), 1894, charcoal and pencil on paper, 24 ½ x 18 ½ inches (62.2 x 47 cm), Image courtesy of the Art Students League of New York

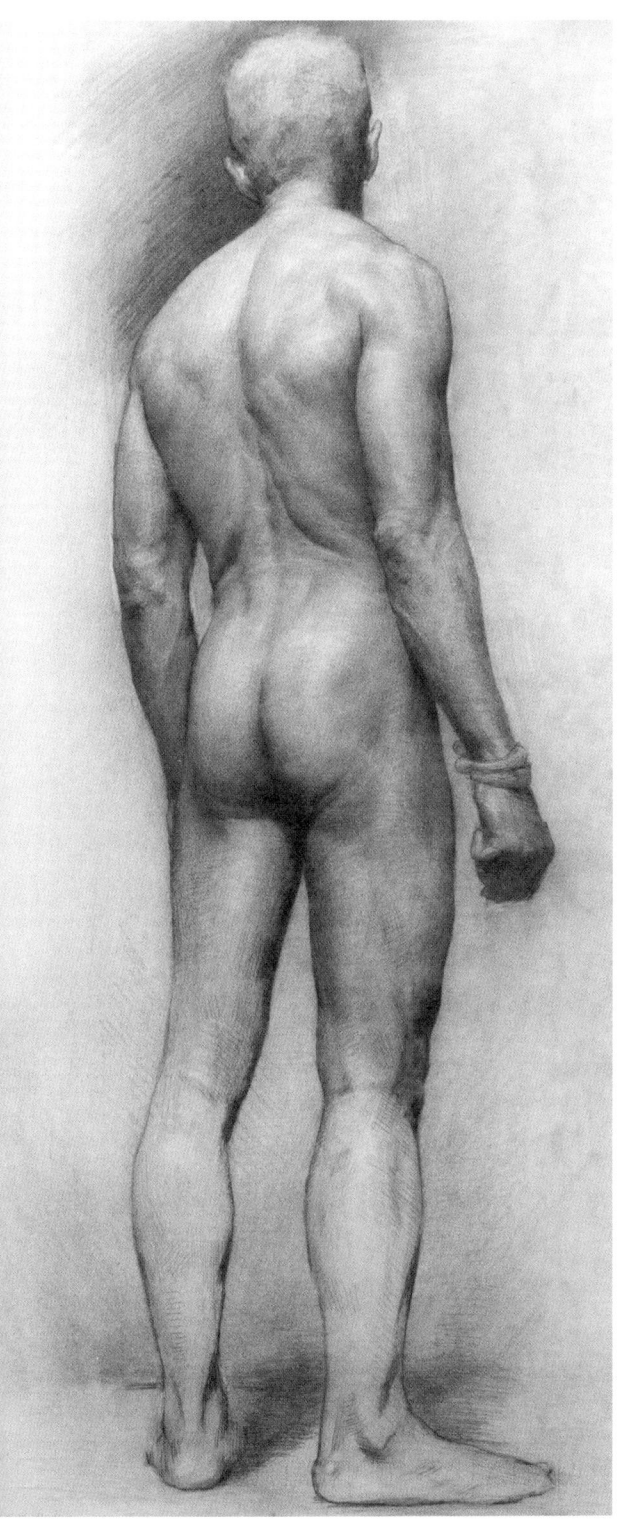

Kevin Muller, *Jimbè*, 2017, graphite on paper,
24 x 18 inches (61 x 45.7 cm)

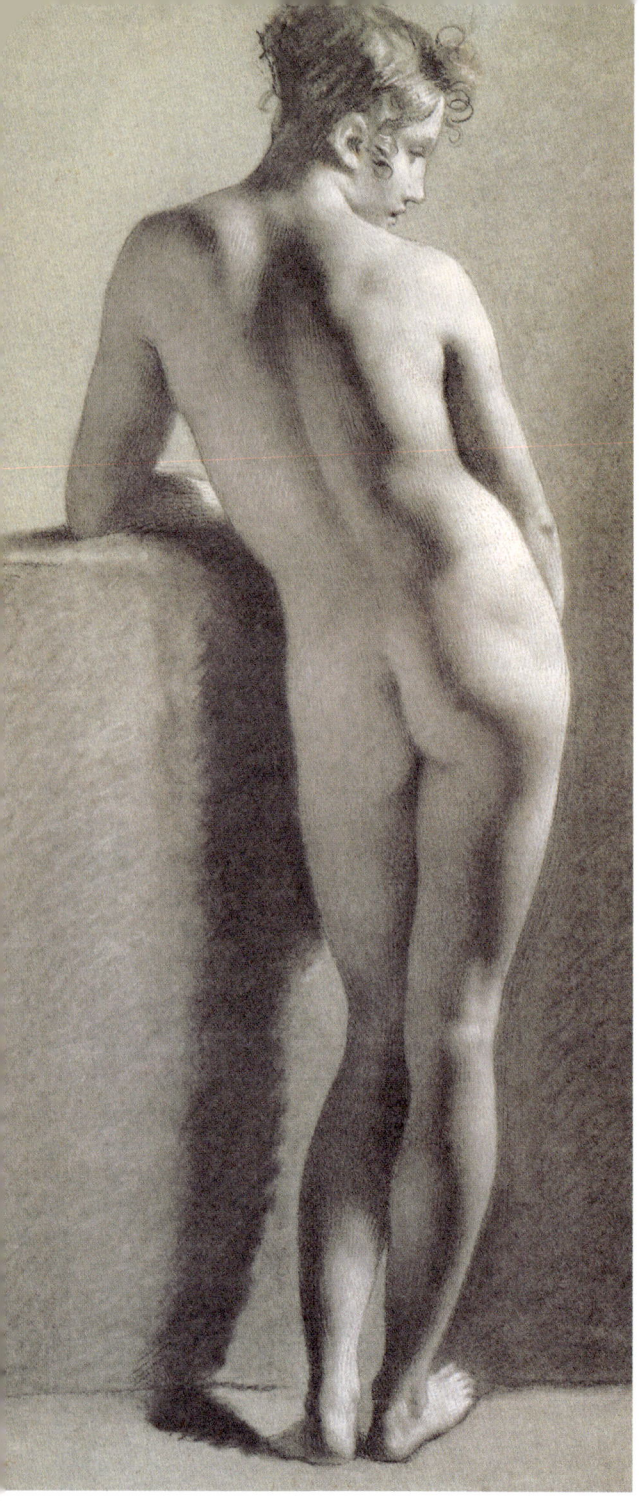

Pierre-Paul Prud'hon, *Standing Female Nude, Seen from Behind,* 1785–90, charcoal heightened with white chalk on blue paper, 24 x 13 ¾ inches (61 x 34.9 cm), Museum of Fine Arts, Boston. Image courtesy of the Art Renewal Center

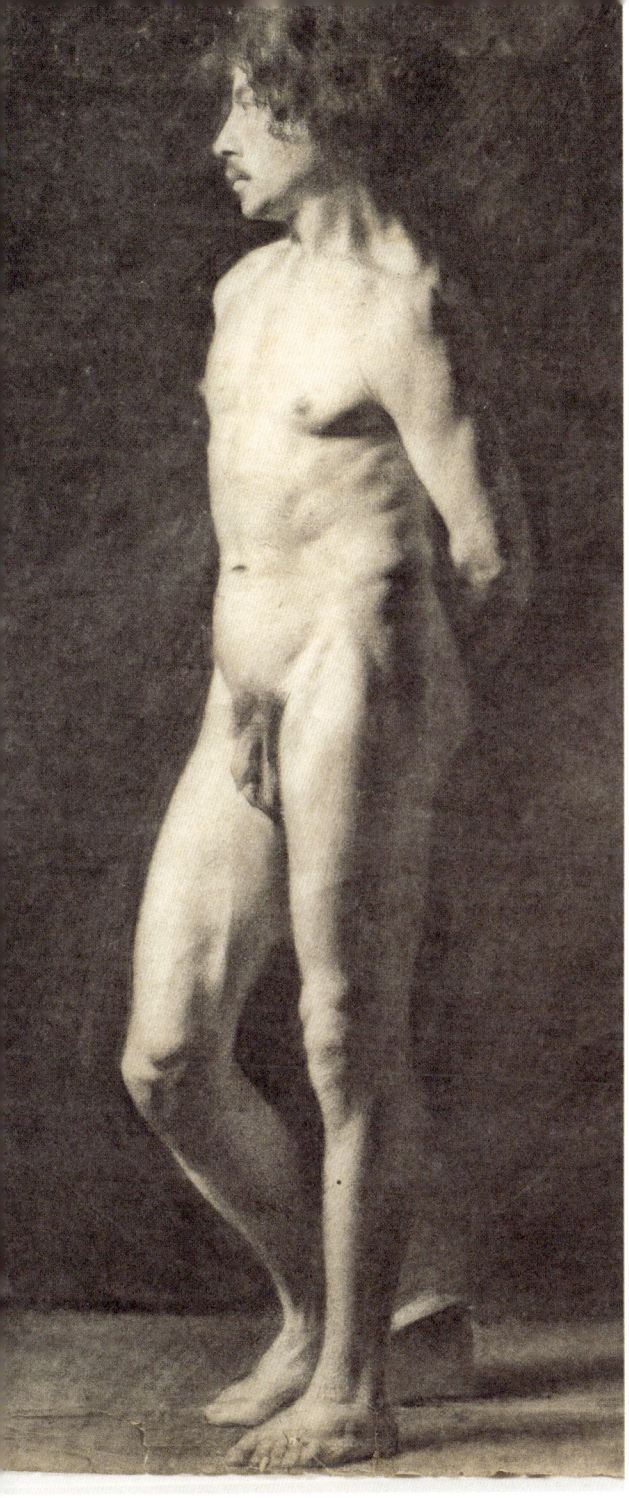

Unknown French artist, Untitled, 19th century, charcoal on paper, 24 x 18 ½ inches (61 x 47 cm), collection of Jordan Sokol and Amaya Gurpide

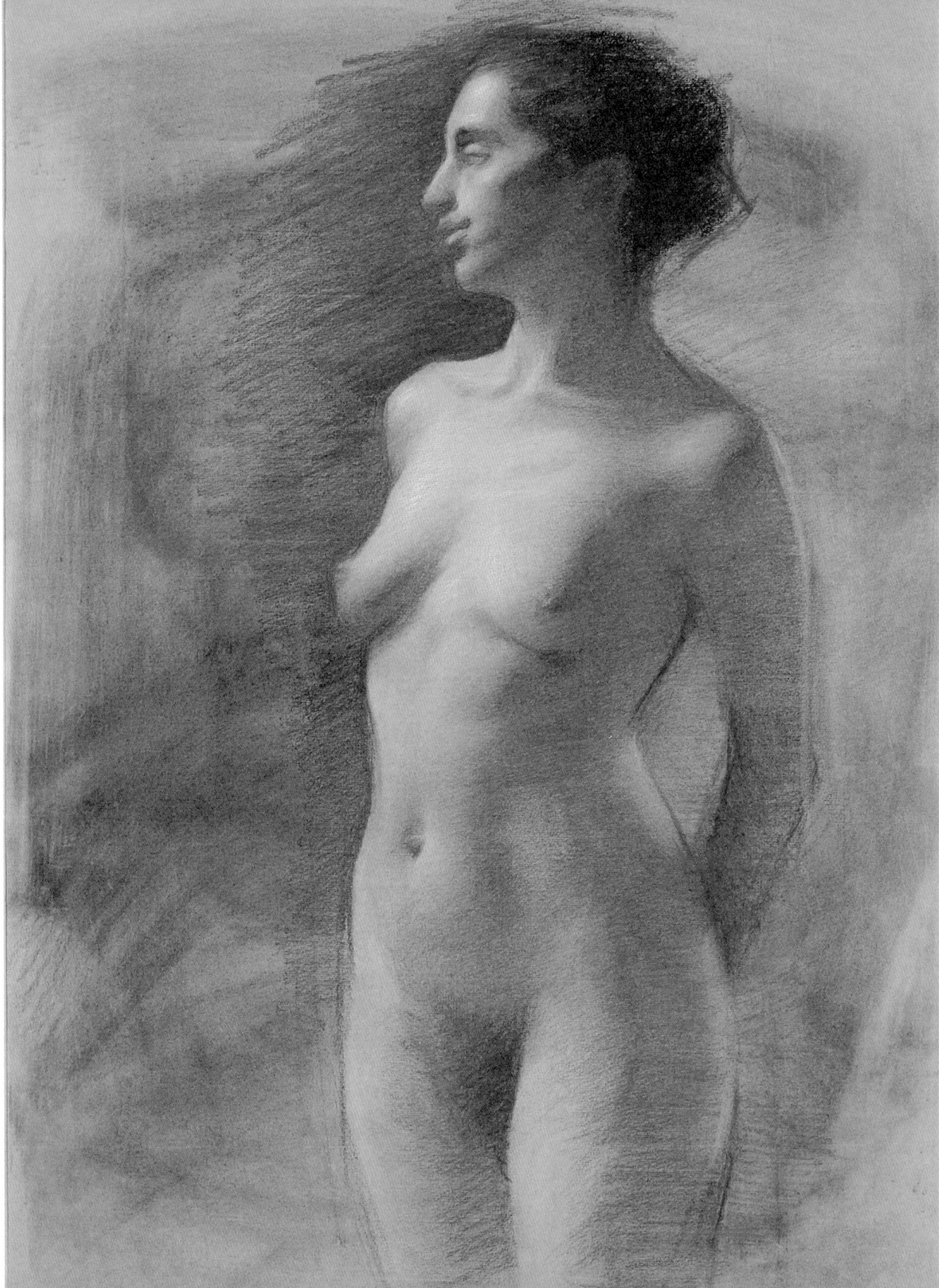

Juliette Aristides, *Adele*, 2015, charcoal on toned paper heightened with white, 24 x 18 inches (61 x 45.7 cm)

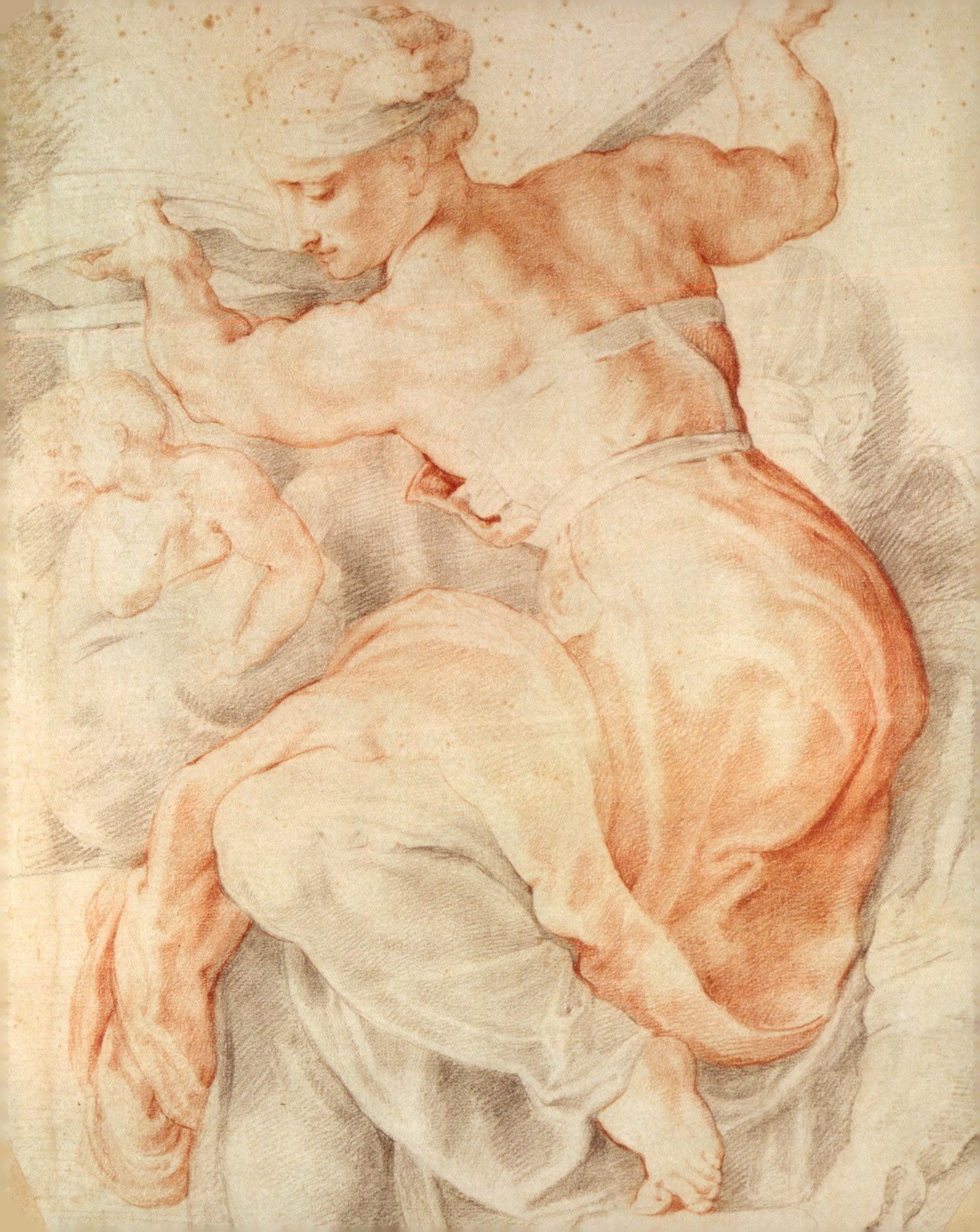

SIX

MASTER STUDIO

I have not made you study the masters that you should copy them.
The studies were indispensable to give you a vocabulary, but now
that you possess it, speak and tell of your own times.
—THOMAS COUTURE, *CONVERSATIONS ON ART METHODS*

One of the easiest ways to learn something new, in any field, is to follow a good example. Erudition through emulation is how children learn to talk, potters to throw their bowls, and musicians to master their instruments. This also happens to be the way many brilliant artists were trained. Art history's greatest minds—Michelangelo, Raphael, da Vinci, Rubens—all studied artworks by other artists through a practice called *master copy*.

The great Romantic artist Eugène Delacroix, famous for his originality, wrote: "Copies, copying. Here lay the education of most of the great masters. They first learned their master's style as an apprentice is taught how to make a knife, without seeking to show their own originality. Afterwards, they copied everything they could lay hands on among the works of the past or contemporary artists."

When artists copy other works, the goal is not necessarily duplication; it is to study from the greats and learn their secrets. When copying, we find ourselves using different lines and forms, making decisions differently than we would on our own, trying new ideas on for size. Over time, we get a storehouse of images and solutions to pull out when we need them. We embody their drawings and add their mastery to our own experience. We get a chance to see through their eyes. Even if you don't plan on becoming a professional artist, you will forever appreciate a work of art more deeply after copying it. All master copies must be correctly attributed. Much historical work can be freely copied after the artist has been dead for 75 years. Contemporary artists may only be copied with the artist's permission.

OPPOSITE: This Rubens drawing is a master copy of Michelangelo's *The Libyan Sybil.*

Peter Paul Rubens, *The Libyan Sibyl, after Michelangelo,* date unknown, black and red chalk, 20 $7/10$ x 13 $3/10$ inches (52.5 x 33.6 cm), Musée du Louvre, Paris. Image courtesy of the Art Renewal Center

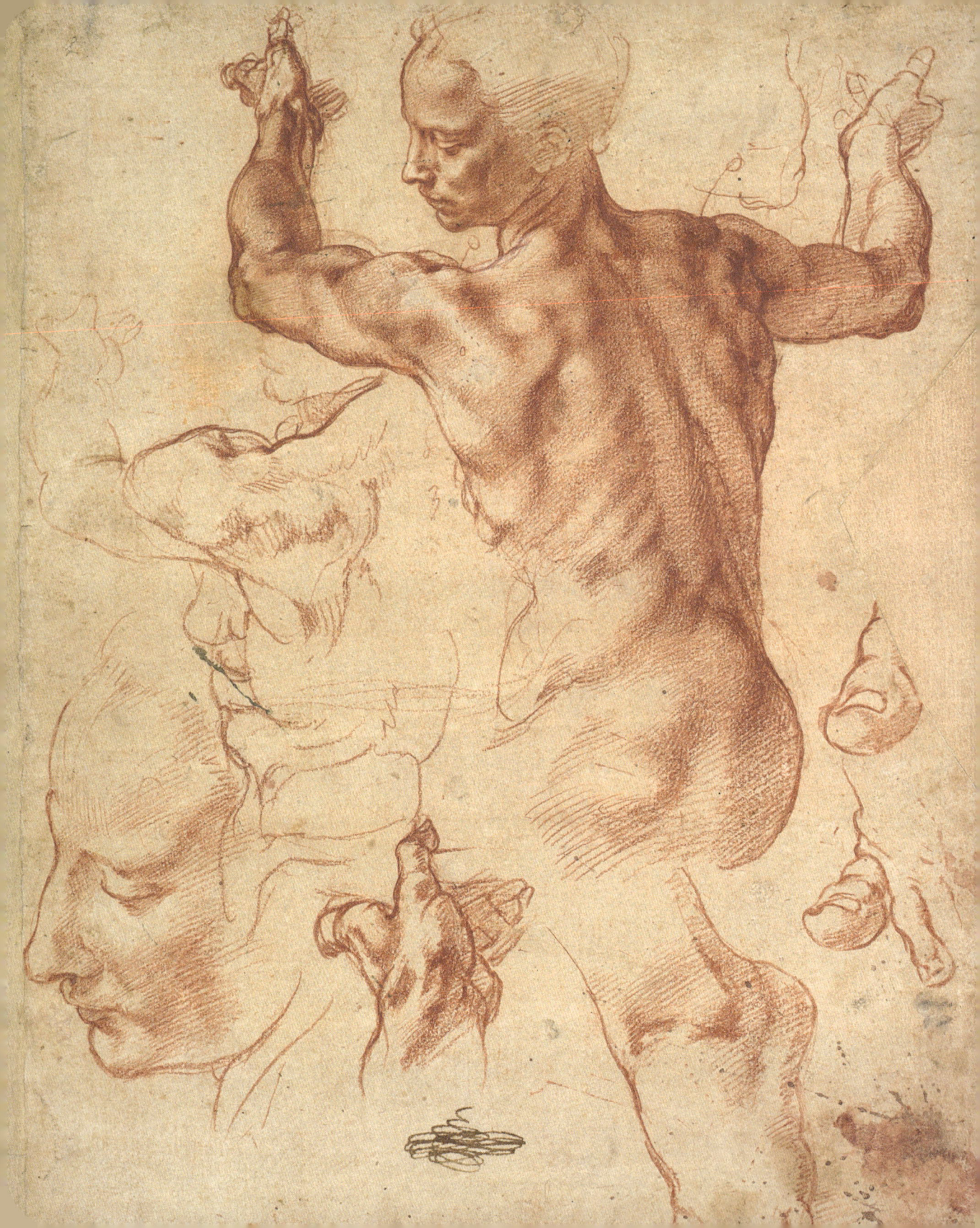

Michelangelo Buonarroti, *Studies for the Libyan Sibyl* (right); *Studies for the Libyan Sibyl and a Small Sketch for a Seated Figure* (left), ca. 1510–11, red chalk, with small accents of white chalk on the left shoulder of the figure in the main study (right); soft black chalk, or less probably charcoal (left), 11 ⅜ x 8 ⁷⁄₁₆ inches (28.9 x 21.4 cm), Metropolitan Museum of Art, New York

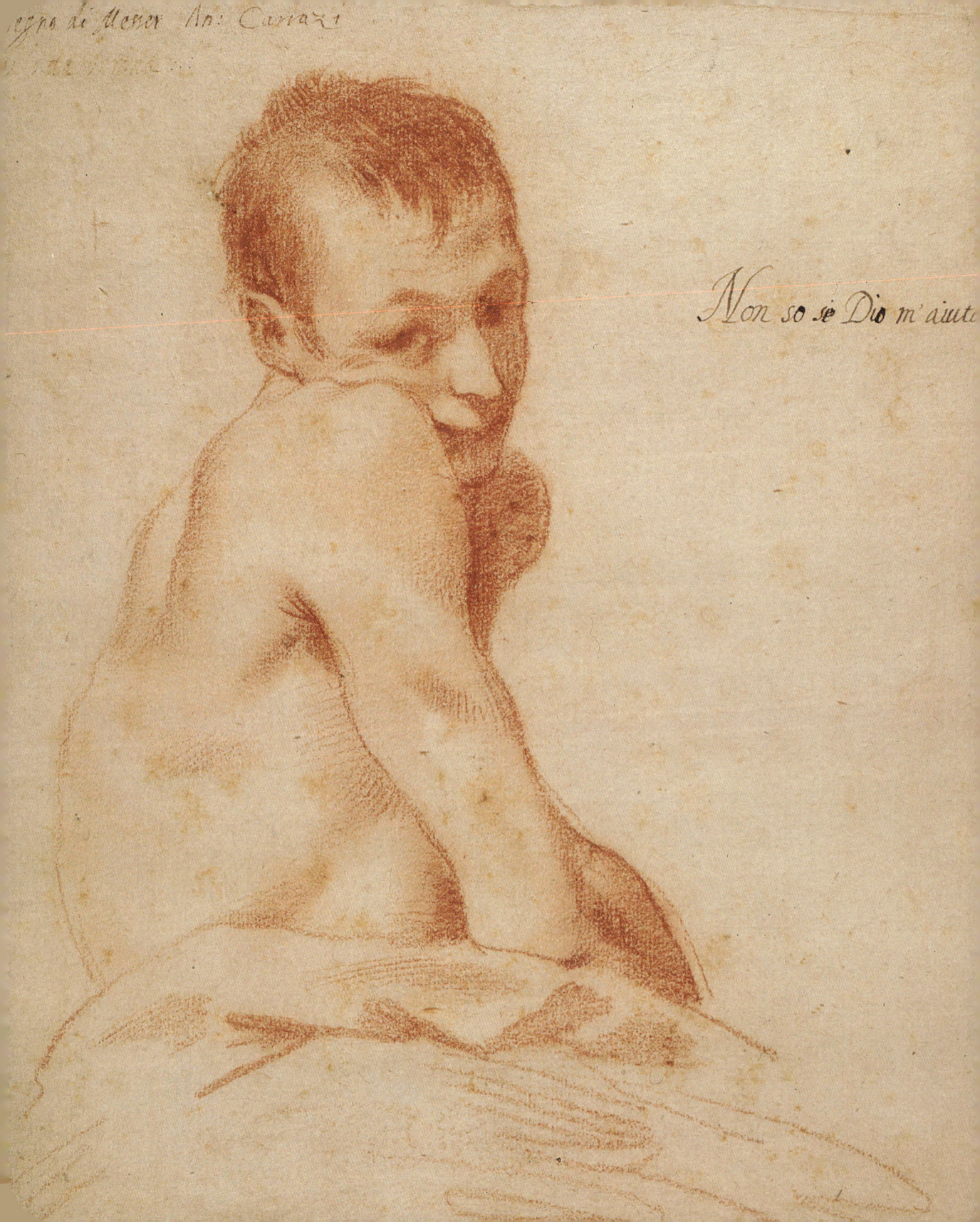

Non so se Dio m'aiute

Annibale Carracci, *A Hunchback Boy,* ca. 1580–90, red chalk with red wash on white paper, Chatsworth House, Derbyshire, England. Image courtesy of the Art Renewal Center

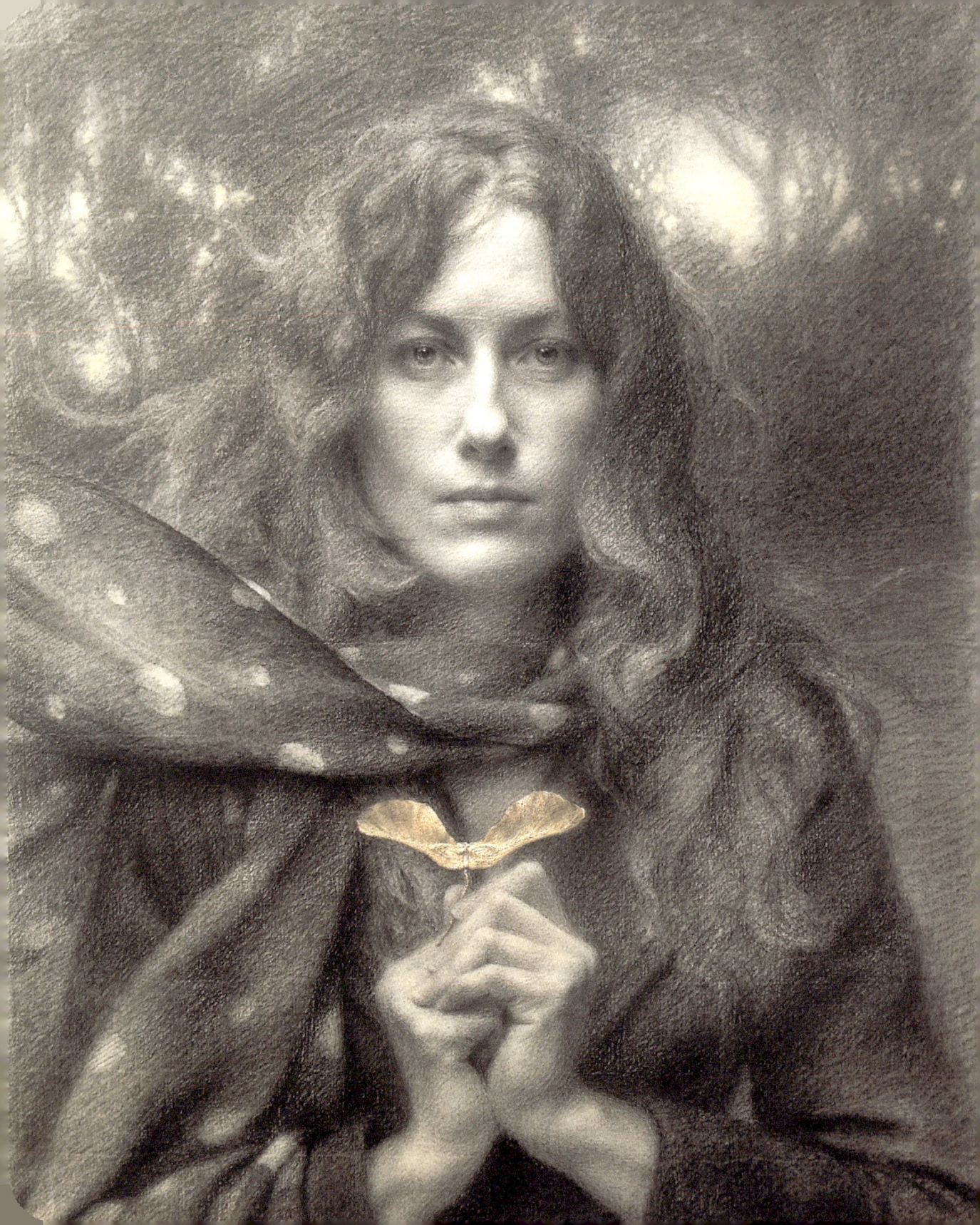

CLOSING

So, in an age of acceleration, nothing can be more exhilarating than going slow. And in an age of distraction, nothing is so luxurious as paying attention. And in an age of constant movement, nothing is so urgent as sitting still.

—PICO IYER

Not all moments in life are equal. There are indelible events, such as the birth of a child, etched in memory, and others that merge together, as quickly forgotten as the long hours of a sleepless night. The importance of a moment is often not connected to *what* is happening but *how* it's experienced.

Once, after a week of rain, rays of golden sunlight shone through my window, hitting my kitchen wall in an iridescent rectangle. I didn't leave the house until the image was imbedded in my mind and the light had faded. The sunlight was a tiny moment of beauty, a natural wonder with the promise of spring, as powerful to me in that moment as any Rembrandt painting. Sublime beauty is experienced when I am alone, and can be elicited by simple things such as a few notes from a piano or raindrops on leaves. Because these moments of awe are highly personal, they are difficult to put into words. Painter Robert Henri said that the times we see beyond the usual "are the moments of our greatest happiness." His words resonate, as I feel most intensely alive during these moments of focused, solitary attention. It is only then that I see the world as an artist.

The desire to record and share this experience of deep seeing is the driving force behind much artistic creation. It enables us to acknowledge the quick passage of time and our desire to make it last, dressing what is fading with a form of immortality, transforming ordinary life into the extraordinary through our attention. Experiences too subtle for normal language can be conveyed through great art. If the artist is successful, we see through his eyes, experiencing what he felt, no matter how long ago he lived.

In modern life, we can sink under the torrent of images. Hundreds of millions of images are uploaded to the internet every day. These images are like moments. They are not necessarily memorable because of their subject or their abundance, but to the degree by which they

---

OPPOSITE: Kamille Corry, *Winter Self-Portrait*, 2014, charcoal, charcoal pencil, and gold pigment on toned paper, 26 x 18 inches (66 x 45.7 cm), private collection

move us. In other words, like a good meal, we remember one image out of a thousand because of our experience of it. I would trade every image that rushes past me for the significant few that make me feel alive or inspired. If focused attention is the key to laying hold of the memorable in life and art, how can we learn to look more deliberately—or, in this case, to see people more memorably?

By learning to draw.

Time spent drawing is an investment in our lives, helping us find beauty in unlikely places. Drawing can make any face or figure worthy of remembering. Figure drawing, in particular, helps us appreciate the body, not because the body is useful, but because it is beautiful. Drawing can, if we let it, show us the beauty of an old woman sitting in a poorly lit subway car, or etch in memory a person lying on a bench. It transforms our lives, recalibrating our vision to see the significant elements hidden in an ordinary day.

This sketchbook was designed to train your eyes to see past the surface, using principles that have trained artists for millennia to see the familiar human figure differently. Learning the principles of drawing can set you on a path of study that lasts a lifetime: not one of knowledge and facts, but of deep encounters with people and places where you live. My hope is that your explorations in drawing enable you to see something new and beautiful in the world.

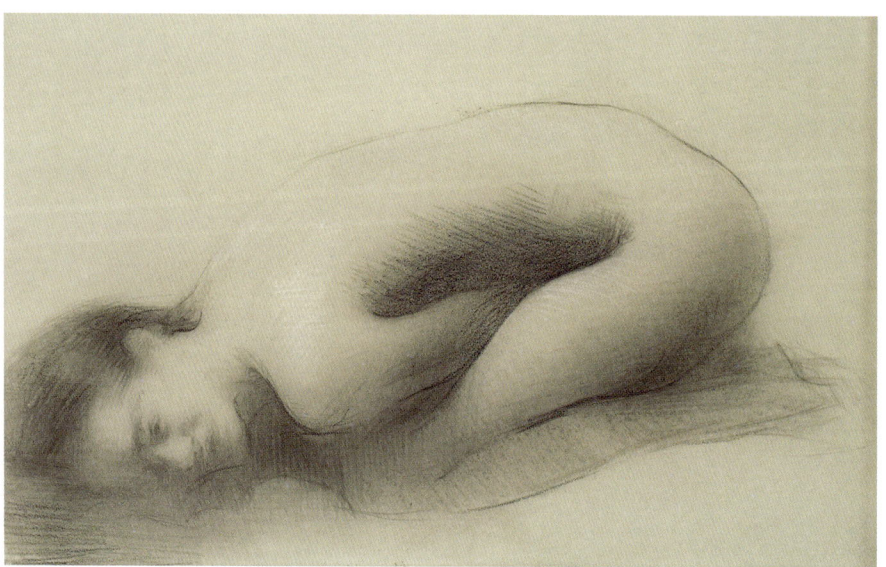

ABOVE: Juliette Aristides, *Figure Sketch*, 2014, Stabilo pencil on glass, 10 x 12 inches (25.4 x 30.5 cm)

OPPOSITE: Yoann Lossel, *The Rise*, 2017, graphite, twenty-four-carat gold and silver leaf on paper, 27 ½ x 19 ½ inches (70 x 50 cm). Image courtesy of the Art Renewal Center

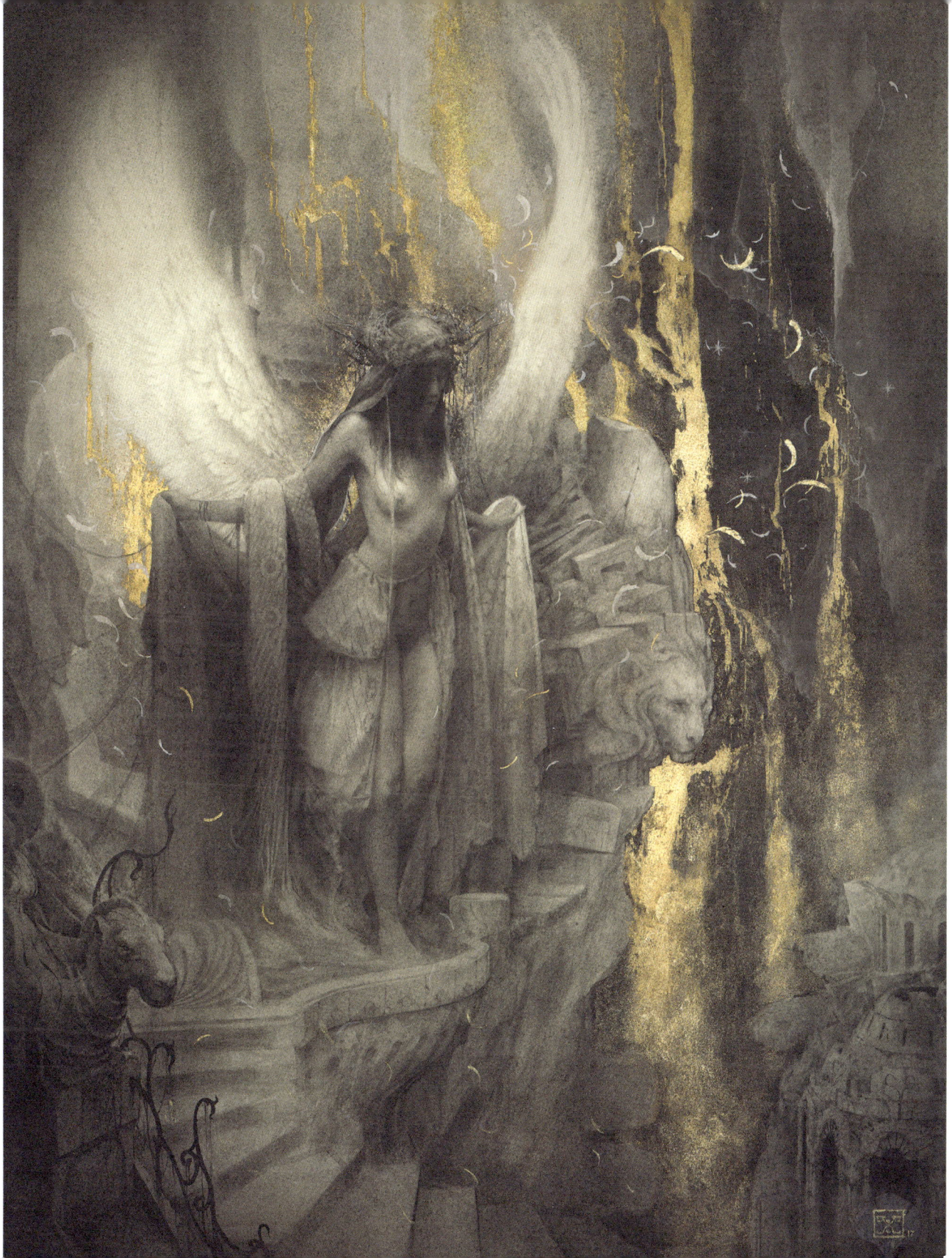

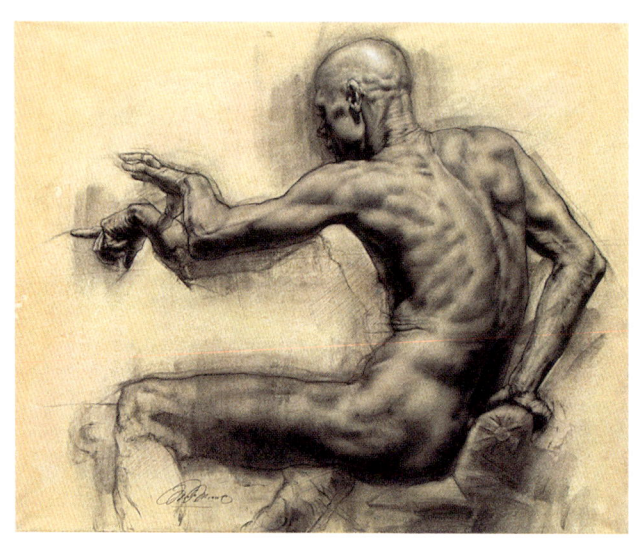

ACKNOWLEDGMENTS

Thank you to the wonderful Victoria Craven, associate publisher at The Monacelli Press, for her belief in me and her confidence in this book. To Ovidio Cartagena, who has art in his bones: working together on image analysis and layout design made a challenging project a pleasure. I am lucky to have worked with editor Julie Mazur Tribe and the elegant, gifted designer Jennifer K. Beal Davis.

This sketchbook could not have been made without the beautiful drawings contributed by many talented and generous artists. I am especially grateful to Candice Bohannon, Michael Mentler, Stan Prokopenko, Joshua Jacobo of New Masters Academy, and Kevin Chen of Concept Design Academy. Thank you to the Metropolitan Museum of Art and the J. Paul Getty Museum for their open-source images, and to the Art Students League of New York for sharing work from its archives. My sincere appreciation to the Art Renewal Center (www. artrenewal.org), especially chairman Fred Ross and cochairman Kara Lysandra Ross, for art permissions and for changing people's lives through the Art Renewal Center. And, of course, thank you to Will Berkowitz. To my parents and family, thank you for your support and love.

Charles Miano, *Reaching Man*, 2014, charcoal on toned paper heightened with white, 20 x 24 inches (50.8 x 61 cm)

INDEX

Page numbers in *italics* indicate illustrations

A

accuracy, checking for, 11, 92
action lines, 12, 17–33
  choosing, 18
  curved, 22, 24
  diagonal, 20
  direction of, 17
  in gesture drawing, 28–30
  repeating, 26
Agar, John Samuel, *13*, 92
anchor points, 11
arcs, 22
Aristides, Juliette, *2*, 4, *11*, *26*, *32*, 92, *93*, 98, *99*, *114*, 115, *124*
armature of figure, 14, 36, 38
Assael, Steven, *16*, 17, *96*, 97

B

Barque, Charles, *38*, 39, 54, 70, *72–73*
Barry, Colleen, *61*, *104*
Bauman, Stephen, *90*, 91
block-in, 13, 14, 35–51
  armature, 38
  of Degas drawing, 40–41
  first stage of, 35
  general to specific, 38–39
  measuring proportion, 44–49
  straight-line, 36–38
  tips and tilts, 38, 42
Bohannon, Candice, 4, *5*

C

Cambiaso, Luca, *52*, 53, 54, *55*
Carracci, Annibale, *22*, *120*, 121
Cartagena, Ovidio, *34*, 35
C curves, 22
centerline, 36, 38
Chen, Kevin, 54, *74*, 75, *80*, 81, *86*
clavicle, 54
conceptual approach, 69
copying, 10–11, 44, 117
core shadow, 92, 100
Corry, Kamille, *122*, 123
Couture, Thomas, 117
Cox, Kenyon, *1*, 4, *39*, *48–49*
cubed figures, 58–67
cubed forms, 56–57, 66
cubes, 53
curved lines, 17, 22, 24
cylinders, 53

D

da Vinci, Leonardo, *46–47*, 46
deep seeing, 123–124
Degas, Edgar, *40–41*
Delacroix, Eugène, 98, 117
diagonal lines, 20
Dürer, Albrecht, 44, *45*

E

Epictetus, 10
erasers, 11

F

Faigin, Gary, 9
feet, 58, 82–85

figure drawing
  centrality of, 9
  conceptual *v.* naturalistic approach to, 69
  materials and supplies, 11
  parts of body, 70–89
  sequential approach to, 12–15
  tips for, 10–11
  See also action lines; block-in; value; volume
Flack, Geoffrey, 55, *60*, *62*
form drawing, 13, 15, 100–115

G

geometric shapes, 53
gesture drawings, 28–30
Goltzius, Hendrick, *24*
Gurpide, Amaya, *106*

H

halftones, 13, 15, 91, 98
Hampton, Michael, *28*
hands, 76–81
Haverkamp-Begemann, Egbert, 69

head
  block-in, 70–76
  measuring, 46
  placement, 58
  planes of, 54
  tips/tilts, 28, 38
height, 58
Henri, Robert, 9, 35, 123
hips
  angle of, 38
  tips/tilts, 12, 36
horizontal lines, 17, 36, 45
Hung, Samuel, *42*

I

Iyer, Pico, 123

J

Jacobo, Joshua, *64–65*

K

knees, 86

L

Laliashvili, Ivan, *108*, 109
Leeds, Damien, *102*
Leonardo da Vinci, *46–47*, 46
Liberace, Robert, *8*, 9
life model, working with, 10, 100
light
  reflected, 92
  and shadow, 91, 98
  spotlight, 100
lines of action. *See* action lines
Lossel, Yoann, 124, *125*

M

master copy, 10–11, 44, 117
materials and supplies, 11
measuring proportion, 44–49
Mentler, Michael, *88*, 89
Michelangelo, *118*, 119
Muller, Kevin, *111*

N

naturalistic approach, 69

O

observational drawing, 69, 98

P

Parkhurst, Daniel, 36
pelvis
    plane of, 55
    tips/tilts, 12, 28, 38, 55–57
pencils, 11
Prokopenko, Stanislav, *56, 76, 78*
proportion, measuring, 44–49
Prud'hon, Pierre-Paul, *112*

R

Raphael, *20*
reflected light, 92
Renaissance art, proportion in, 44
ribcage
    mass of, 54
    plane of, 54–55

tips/tilts, 28, 36, 38, 55–57
Rilke, Rainer Maria, 91
Rubens, Peter Paul, 20, *21, 66, 67, 68,* 69, *116,* 117
Rubenstein, Ephraim, *94–95*

S

Sargent, John Singer, *34,* 35
Schiavonetti, Luigi, 26, *27*
S curves, 24
serpentine lines, 24
shadow
    core, 92, 100
    and light, 91, 98
    mapping, 13, 15
shadow shapes, 14, 92, 94
shoulders
    angle of, 36
    plane of, 54
    tips/tilts, 12, 55
Sijben de Maroye, Marcel, 22, *23*
Sims, Tenaya, *15,* 92
slow seeing, 98

Speed, Harold, 36, *37,* 53, 92
spheres, 53
spotlight, 100
Steele, Alexey, 5, *6,* 98
straight lines, 17
    block-in, 36–38
    shadow shapes, 100

T

Tack, Augustus Vincent, *50*
Thoreau, Henry David, 18
tips and tilts, 12, 28, 38, 42, 55–57
tone. *See* value
Tweedy, Richard, *110*

V

value
    defined, 91
    gradation, 92
    and halftones, 98
    mapping, 92–97
    rendering form, 100–115
value step scale, 102, *103*

vertical lines, 17, 36, 45
Villon, Jaques, 17
Vilppu, Glen, *30, 59, 82, 84*
volume, 52–67
    in cubed figures, 58–67
    in cubed forms, 56–57
    in geometric shapes, 53
    masses of body, 54–55
    and reflected light, 92

W

Werner, Robin, *38,* 39

Z

Zuccaro, Taddeo, 18, *19*

ABOUT THE AUTHOR

Juliette Aristides is an extraordinary draftsperson and artist with a deep and well-rounded education. She studied at the Pennsylvania Academy of the Fine Arts, the National Academy of Design, and various private ateliers, and is the director of the Aristides Atelier in Seattle, Washington, at Gage Academy of Fine Art (since 2000). Aristides exhibits in one-person and group shows nationally. Aristides is also the best-selling author of *Beginning Drawing Atelier*, *Classical Drawing Atelier*, *Classical Painting Atelier*, *Lessons in Classical Drawing*, and *Lessons in Classical Painting*. She is based in Seattle. For more about the artist, visit her website at AristidesArts.com.

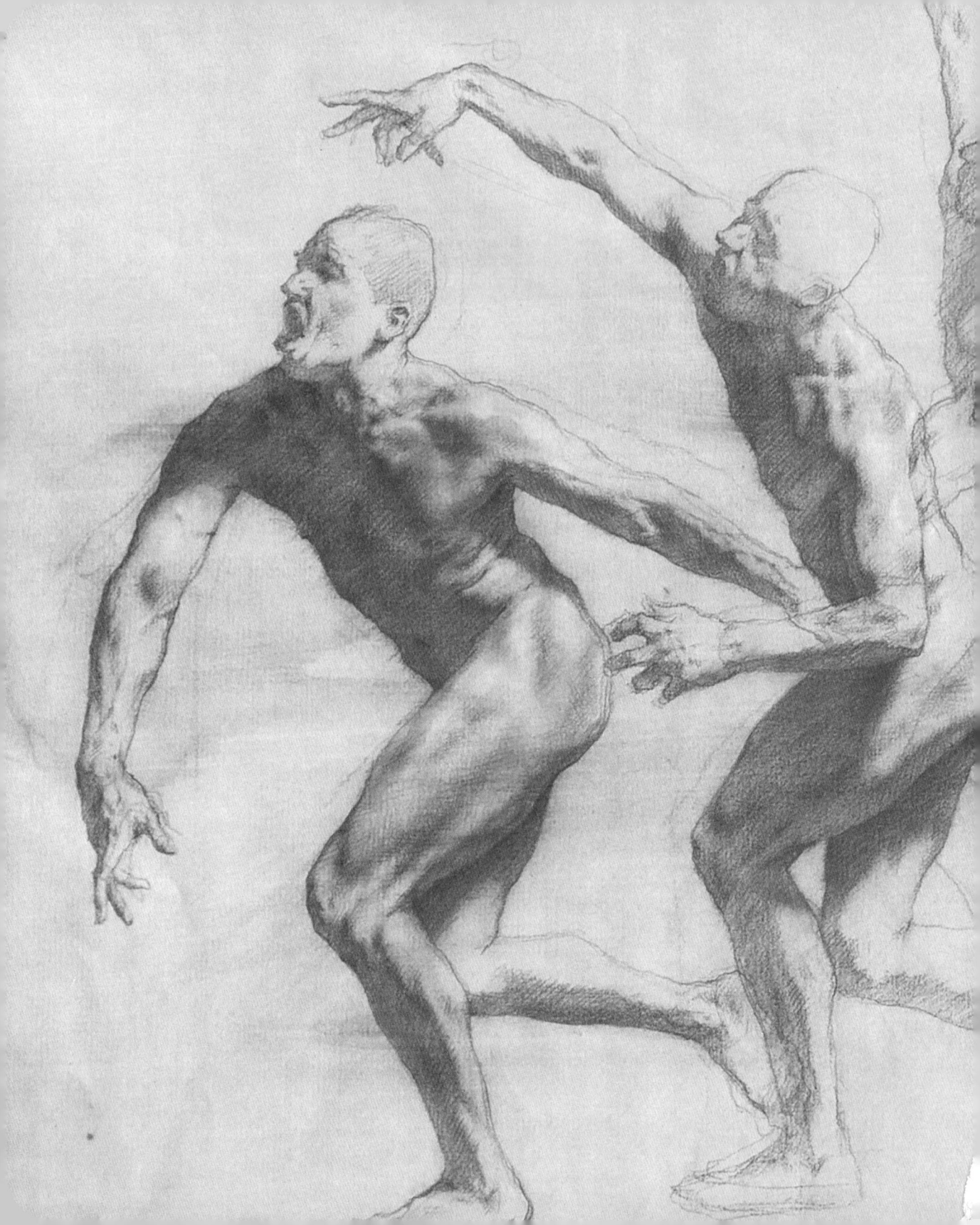